Index

- Contents 2
- Components 4
- Introduction 8
- Celebrations 24
- Flashcard games 25
- Traditional stories 28
- Audio transcripts 60
- Unit worksheets 81
- Celebration worksheets .. 135
- Certificate 141
- Letters to parents 142
- Evaluations 151
- Term dividers 154
- Main characters for colouring 157

Contents

At school
Tina's chair

Page 37

New: picture, table, chair
Review: pencil, rubber, paper, crayon, book, teacher, floor; red, blue, yellow, green; bird, whale, duck, frog; 1–3; circle, square
Photo poster: A Ugandan school – *school, classroom, playground, writing, reading*
Authentic song: Tommy Thumb

My family
Petal's family

Page 41

New: sofa, bed, bath
Review: brother, sister, grandad, mummy, daddy, baby, granny; red, blue, green, yellow, black, white, brown; bird, whale, frog, duck, hen, mouse, bear; 1–5; circle, square, triangle
Photo poster: My family all help – *feeding the cat, making the bed, laying the table, walking the dog, watering the plants*
Authentic song: Five little ducks

My body
The snowman

Page 45

New: hair, hands, feet; long, short; giraffe, penguin
Review: arm, leg, head, eyes, ears, nose, mouth; red, blue, green, yellow, orange, black, white, brown; bird, whale, frog, duck, fish, hen, mouse, bear; 1–5; circle, square, triangle; big, little, mouse, mosquito
Photo poster: It's Christmas! – *Christmas card, cracker, paper hat, turkey, Christmas pudding*
Authentic song: The little bells of Christmas

Toys
What a mess!

Page 49

New: robot, game, scooter
Review: slide, swing, bike, ball, dolly, teddy, monster; red, blue, green, yellow, orange, black, white, pink, brown, purple; bird, whale, frog, duck, fish, hen, mouse, pig, bear, snake; 1–6; circle, square, triangle, rectangle
Photo poster: Exercise makes us strong – *climbing, skipping, playing football, cycling, swimming*
Authentic song: One finger, one thumb

Clothes
I'm Tommy's parrot

Page 53

New: socks, shoes, jumper; seven; on, under
Review: trousers, shirt, dress, hat, jacket, boots, scarf; red, blue, green, yellow, orange, black, white, pink, brown, purple; 1–6; circle, square, triangle, rectangle
Photo poster: Different materials – *gloves, wool, cotton, pyjamas, leather*
Authentic song: She'll be coming round the mountain

Contents

Around town
Tommy's a wonderful tiger

Page 57

New: hospital, school, shop; loud, quiet; eight
Review: police officer, fire fighter, doctor; car, bus, train, plane; red, blue, green, yellow, orange, black, white, pink, brown, purple; 1–7
Photo poster: Posting a letter – *letter box, letter, post man, post office, post box*
Authentic song: The wheels on the bus

Food
Wash your hands, please

Page 61

New: cheese, ham, tomato, pizza; in, next to; nine
Review: biscuit, sandwich, yoghurt, apple, banana, pear, orange; red, blue, green, yellow, orange, black, white, pink, brown, purple; 1–8; long, short, loud, quiet; on, under
Photo poster: Are your snacks healthy? – *buns, sweets, crisps, nuts, fruit*
Authentic song: Today is Monday

Animals
I'm sad! I'm grumpy! I'm sleepy!

Page 65

New: lion, bear, monkey; in front of, behind; ten
Review: cat, fish, dog, cow, pig, sheep, chicken; red, blue, yellow, green, orange, black, white, pink, brown, purple; 1–9; circle, square, triangle, rectangle; on, under, in, next to
Photo poster: Creepy crawlies – *butterfly, fly, spider, ladybird, bee*
Authentic song: There was an old lady

Outside
Magic sky

Page 69

New: rainbow, star, moon
Review: mountain, sea, beach, river, flower, tree, sun; red, blue, green, yellow, orange, black, white, pink, brown, purple; bird, whale, frog, duck, fish, hen, mouse, pig, bear, snake; 1–10; circle, square, triangle, rectangle; on, under, in, next to, in front of, behind; long, short, loud, quiet
Photo poster: Our day – *day, night, firework, bat, owl*
Authentic song: I can sing a rainbow

3

Student's material

Big Jungle Fun's Student's Book consists of 54 eye-catching worksheets in full colour, stickers, 12 enjoyable pop-outs and a multi-ROM.

Worksheets
Each worksheet introduces the vocabulary and the concepts in a visual way, with activities aimed at the development of skills appropriate to their age, such as colouring, tracing, drawing, glueing, relating, identifying, making sequences and counting.

Using these worksheets, the teacher can monitor the development of the class using the main activities, like a song, a story or a poster.

On the reverse of each worksheet you can find the instructions in English and an optional creative activity.

Activity Book
The Activity Book offers extra activities to reinforce the main course content in a fun way. There are also worksheets for each story in the Traditional Story Big Book. The children can use the worksheets to create their own version of the story.

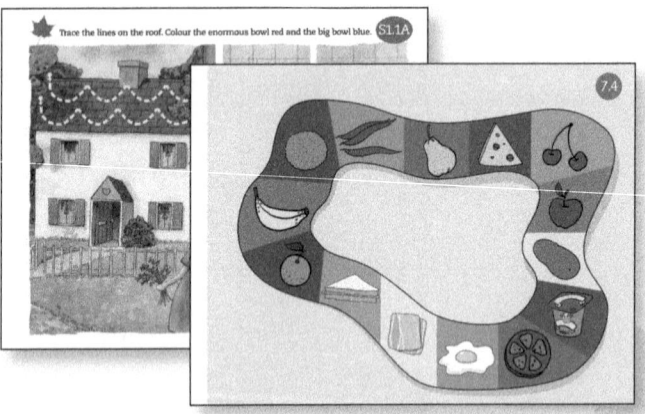

Multi-ROM
This CD contains a selection of the songs from the course so that the children can listen to and sing them at home. It also contains the children's version of the three traditional stories, as well as entertaining computer games to practise the main vocabulary.

Pop-outs
An envelope with 9 full colour pop-outs to be used in lessons 4 that the children can manage easily. There are 3 extra pop-outs of the characters that can be used during games, the stories or songs.

Stickers
An envelope with attractive stickers for lessons 1, 4 and 6 of each unit. There are also *gomets* for various activities and stickers to congratulate the children on their work.

Teacher's material

Puppets
You can use the soft toys Tommy and Tina and the glove puppet Polly to help the children learn the English language. Through these toys, the teacher can introduce vocabulary in an enjoyable way.

Flashcards and Jungle cube
There is a corresponding illustrated card for each new word. The flashcards are a useful tool to introduce and review vocabulary. The reverse of every card shows the level and the unit it belongs to. The teacher's guide offers many games and ideas about how to use these cards to help the children with their learning. (For more information about the *Jungle Cube* please go to page 21.)

Photo posters
A poster with images from the real world corresponding to Lesson 6 of each unit. The perfect opportunity to revise the vocabulary from the unit in an alternative way.

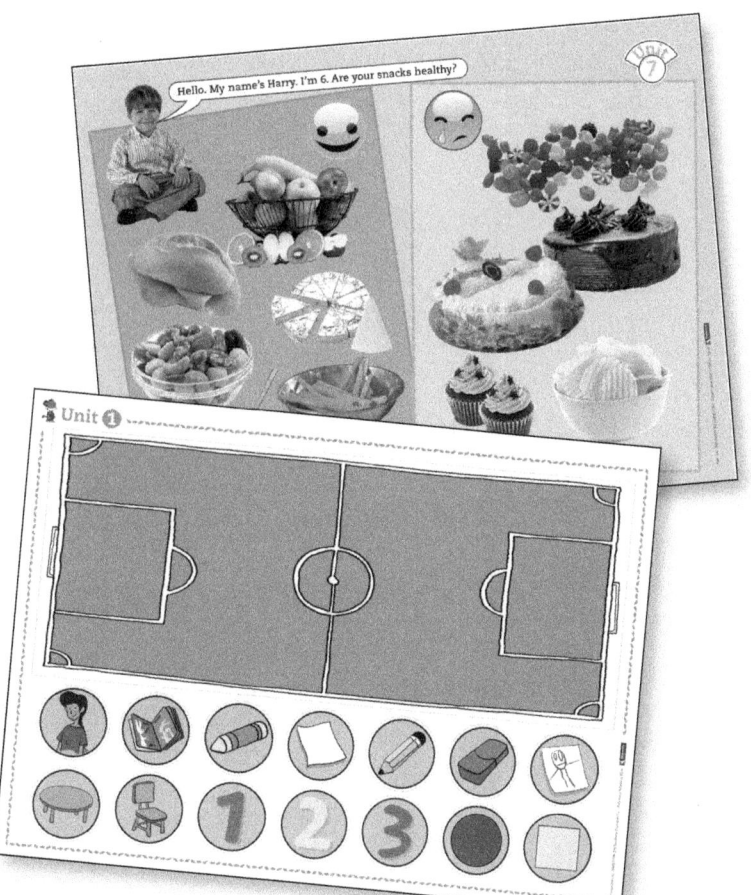

Story cards
72 full colour story cards: 9 tales and 8 cards per tale. Each story card shows the corresponding text on the reverse.
Use the story cards to tell the story, practise the vocabulary and to sequence, predict and describe everything that happens in the story.

Posters
Within each unit there is a pop-out poster which can be used to practise the vocabulary and concepts in an interactive and fun way.

Teacher's material

Teacher's Book
This guide is a large version of the student's worksheet to be used as a template for the class. It helps to review the vocabulary from the songs and stories and also explains what the students need to do. The reverse of the worksheet offers step by step instructions for the lesson as well as the necessary material. Each lesson also includes an optional activity and the corresponding Basic Competence.

Teacher's Resource Book
54 photocopiable worksheets for the B Lessons. It also includes the complete audio transcript, general information, teaching notes for the traditional stories, extra activities for special celebrations, evaluation sheets, letters for parents and a diploma.

Traditional Stories Big Book and CD
Three traditional stories beautifully illustrated in one huge book. Each story has been carefully written to focus on the vocabulary in *Big Jungle Fun*. The first story relates to units 1 and 2; the second to units 4, 5 and 6 and the third to units 7, 8 and 9. On pages 28 to 56 you can find ideas about how to present the story as well as a series of activities that can be done as the story is being told, as well as after having listened to it. The corresponding worksheets are at the back of the Activity Book. Each story also has a worksheet to relate its contents to the real world as well as a creative worksheet to encourage participation.

Big Book and CD
A huge story book containing four new stories with Tommy, Tina and Polly. Through this book, children will practise basic concepts like colours, numbers, geometric shapes and positions of objects, as well as the course vocabulary.

Class CD
The complete recording of all the songs, stories and musical games.

Teacher's digital material

Animated stories DVD
There is an alternative way to present the stories to the class: animated stories. The children can watch the stories come to life and listen to their friends' adventures. The cartoons can be shown on a DVD player, on a PC or on an interactive whiteboard.

Big Book Story Activities
A CD-ROM with animated versions of the *Big Book* stories. It can be played on an interactive whiteboard or a PC. The cartoons include hidden actions that the children can have fun discovering.

Multi-ROM
Didactic computer games to practise the course language and content.

Activity Generator
An ingenious tool for teachers which offers the possibility of creating personalised worksheets using the *Big Jungle Fun* material. The Activity Generator allows the content of the photocopiable worksheets to be rearranged and edited to create new worksheets, supporting the needs of each class and each moment.

IWB Activities
This enjoyable tool is designed to be used on the interactive whiteboard and provides the teacher with an innovative way to approach the *Big Jungle Fun* course contents. Each unit includes two interactive activities based on the main course vocabulary and concepts. The audio allows the children to listen to the instructions in English, while the activities offer the teacher a wide variety of tools to help improve the students' learning process.

Flashcard Bank
The electronic version of the course flashcards. This tool allows the teacher to combine the flashcards to create personalised selections. It includes an audio option allowing the children to listen to each word on the flashcard and practise the pronunciation, as well as the possibility of seeing the written word. These flashcards can be printed in full colour or in black and white, to be coloured by students. The flashcard bank can be used on a PC as well as an interactive whiteboard.

 Use of digital skills and information

Through the use of digital tools, the children learn about new technologies in the classroom and develop useful skills to help them with their future learning. The children learn and become familiar with IT codes in a natural way, through games. By using interactive tools, they understand the basic functions of the digital board and the computer, and they develop sufficient skills to become progressively more autonomous in their use of these tools within the classroom.

Objectives and methodology

GENERAL OBJECTIVES OF *Big Jungle Fun*

- To offer a meaningful, enjoyable and attractive first contact with the English language.
- To use English as a second language for communication.
- To inspire a sensitivity in children towards English sounds and patterns of communication.
- To complement and enrich the children's education in other areas.
- To ensure that it is a positive and enriching experience for all.

METHODOLOGY OF *Big Jungle Fun*

1. **Language acquisition**
   At a very early age, we acquire a second language in a very similar way to our mother tongue. It is a natural process: the child understands what is being communicated without the need for a translation. The course methodology is directly based in and supported by the same characteristics as the mother tongue acquisition, which are the following:

   * *Mother tongue acquisition develops at the same time as intellectual, physical, emotional and social learning.*

   * *There is a purpose, an aim, to the use of language.*

   * *The children develop their capacity to listen to a language when they are exposed to it, but not put under pressure to speak it.*

   * *Adults generally use very simple vocabulary with children and would automatically include repetitions and pet phrases. This leads the child to naturally repeat the sequence of sounds they are hearing and associate it to something specific.*

   Each unit includes four new vocabulary words and a new concept. However, during the classes, through the teacher's instructions, the songs, stories and activities, the children are exposed to a much wider range of vocabulary and language, and they respond to it in a very natural way.

2. **Importance of context**
   In order to achieve the above objectives, every teaching and learning process needs to be presented in a specific context. In *Big Jungle Fun* this context is presented through the adventures of Tommy, Tina and Polly. As the children identify with the characters, an emotional link is created, stimulating their imagination and giving meaning to the words.

Objectives and methodology

3. **Importance of movement**
   Children's learning process during this phase is basically kinaesthetic: they learn through touch, action and movement.
   * The course connects their learning with the development of motor skills. Through action games and dances, the children develop control over different parts of their body.
   * Manipulating pop-outs, using stickers, linking dots with a line, colouring, sticking *gomets* in specific places, and so on, are all activities that develop the children's fine motor skills and their manual and visual coordination.

4. **Importance of music and rhythm**
   Music is very important for children this age because it helps them develop emotional intelligence and, according to research, children learn better through music and rhythm. In this course children will have access to a selected variety of music, including classical, folk, traditional and pop.
   * All classes and lessons are structured around the songs.
   * Each lesson starts with music, listening or singing one of the songs that has previously been learnt.
   * TPR songs (with actions) in each unit include vocabulary that the children are learning.
   * Numbers, shapes, colours, prepositions and *cross curricular* concepts are reviewed through songs.
   * Each unit includes an activity that requires listening to music and representing certain songs: they are the story chants, rhyming tales that review vocabulary through repetition.

Structure

Big Jungle Fun is designed to be used in a flexible way and to allow the teacher to choose the appropriate activities for each class and each moment.

Every unit is divided into six lessons, where each lesson has an important function within the children's learning process. In the following pages we will show you how this method is organised into lessons.

Step-by-step

Lesson 1 A  An introduction to the unit vocabulary

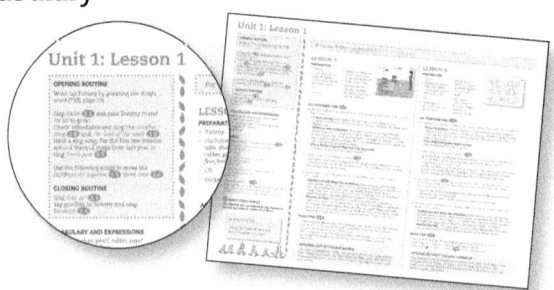

Opening routine
The children wake up Tommy and sing together. Some of the songs are chosen to encourage the children to tune in to the English language. Also, by singing the same songs over and over, the children learn the words in a natural way. As well as that, children can also guess the magic word (see page 19).

Playing with Tommy
The new vocabulary is presented to the children using flashcards and games, with the help of the characters. You'll find details of the flashcard games on pages 25.

Action song
The children listen to a fun song and accompany it with games, gestures and interpretations: a great way to reinforce language through fun.

I can paint a picture, picture, picture,
I can paint a picture. Look at me!

Worksheet
Stickers are used in this lesson. The marks where the stickers are to be stuck are not normally shown on the children's version of the worksheet so that they have to think about where they need to stick them or refer to the teacher's worksheet. This helps to develop logical dexterity.

On the back of the worksheet there are instructions in English and an optional activity that helps to develop the pupil's creative expression.

Lesson 1 B

This lesson is intended for those teachers who give more hours of class or for those who want to practise the vocabulary, expressions or the song that has been learnt in other contexts.

Tommy's music
A musical game with actions which the children listen to and then perform using mime.

Photocopiable worksheet
These worksheets practise the same vocabulary as in Lesson A, but in a different context.

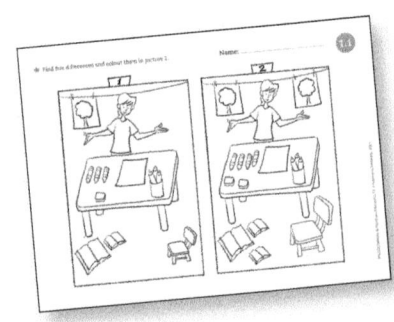

Step-by-step

Lesson 2 A  The basic concepts of the unit

Opening routine
The children wake up Tina and sing the songs together. Music and songs are a great help in class as they help children to memorise the vocabulary in a fun and natural way.

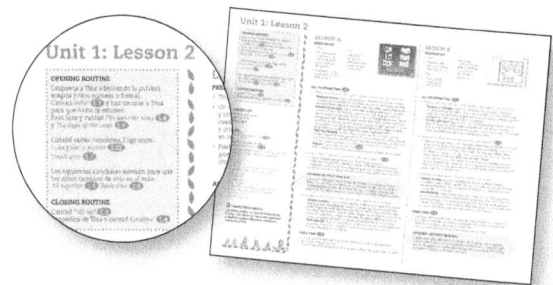

Playing with Tina
Present new concepts to the class, like numbers, colours, sizes or geometric figures through the use of flashcards and games.

Song
Each concept is accompanied by a song to help the children learn and understand it.

Do you know your numbers, numbers, numbers?
Do you know your numbers? Let me see.

Worksheet
The new concept is practised in this worksheet. The instructions are written in English on the back and the optional activity offers further practice.

 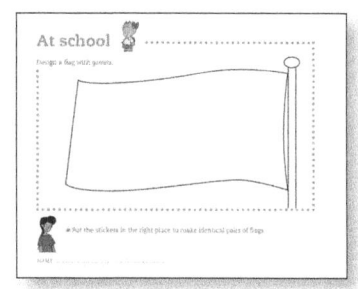

Lesson 2 B

This lesson is intended for those teachers who give more hours of class or for those who want to practise the concepts of the lesson or the song in other contexts.

Photocopiable worksheet
These worksheets practise the same vocabulary and concepts as in lesson A.

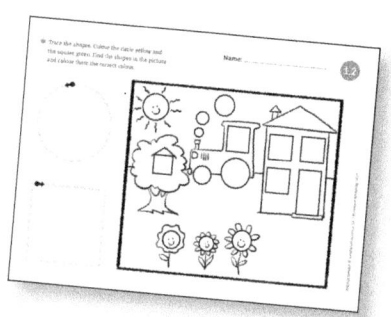

Step-by-step

Lesson 3 A  The story

Opening routine
The children wake up Tommy, Tina and Polly and sing together. Singing in English helps them to gain confidence in the language. We suggest that the songs be used to start the school routine, but they can be enjoyed at any moment.

Playing with Tommy, Tina and Polly
A fun revision of the unit's vocabulary that prepares the children for the story.

Story
The story is told using the story cards and the audio CD. The story's themes are always related to the unit, reinforcing the learning of the concepts and vocabulary. The stories often contain social values that the teacher can easily develop; they are based on the close and affectionate relationships between the three friends who are the main characters of the method.

> We recommend telling and listening to the children's favourite stories several times, since they will probably become increasingly more familiar with the language.

Worksheet
Activities based on the story. There are two worksheets for this lesson; the first one is for cutting and gluing onto the second one.

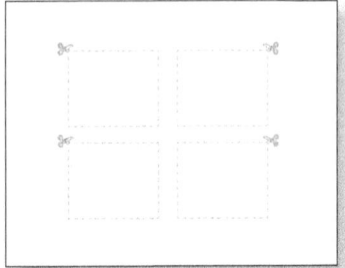

Lesson 3 B

Another lesson for the children to practise the story's vocabulary in a different context.

Story chant
A fun way to repeat the story's main language.

*Tina's on the floor.
Boo, hoo! Boo, hoo!
Don't cry Tina.*

Photocopiable worksheet
More activities for practising the story's vocabulary and the concepts that have been learnt.

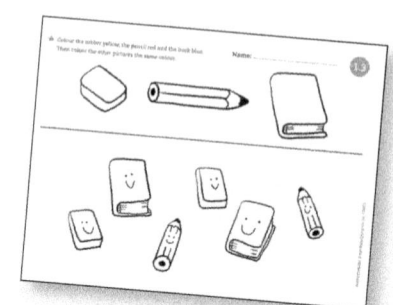

Step-by-step

Lesson 4 A  A variety of activities to review the most important ideas and vocabulary seen up to now

Opening routine
The children wake up Tommy, Tina and Polly and sing together. Singing the songs from previous lessons or units develops the capacity for memorizing, and it is a fun activity for the children.

Playing with Tommy, Tina and Polly
The class goes over the vocabulary and concepts from the unit in a fun way – by playing!

Poster
An interactive resource, which offers the opportunity to recycle and consolidate the vocabulary and concepts from the unit. This gives the children an opporunity to demonstrate their knowledge and allows the teacher to evaluate their understanding. The class shows that it is capable of following simple instructions using the vocabulary from the unit.

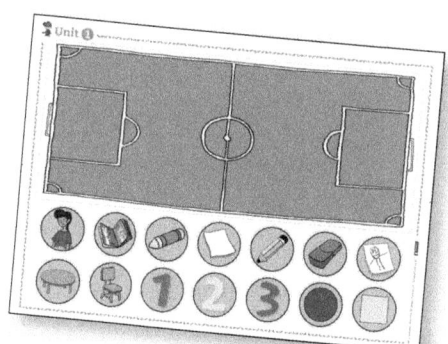

> These posters are not used in the teacher's notes until lesson 4,
> but they can be used at any time.

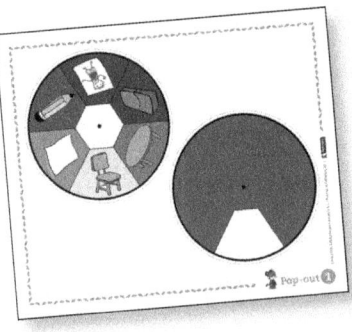

Pop-outs
The children's pop-outs can also be used to check what they have learnt. The children play with them and show co-operation and understanding.

Worksheet
Use the worksheet to go over the vocabulary and language from the unit.

Lesson 4 B  Continuous assessment

In this lesson the children take part in more games and learn whilst using the vocabulary and concepts from the unit, as well as listening to and enjoying the songs and stories.

Photocopiable worksheet
This worksheet is an ideal way to check the children's understanding of everything they have practised throughout the unit so far. It is always much better to evaluate the children in small groups so that the teacher can easily observe how each child completes each of the activities. This will help the teacher to evaluate what each child has learnt. There is also the option of listening to the instructions on the Class CD.

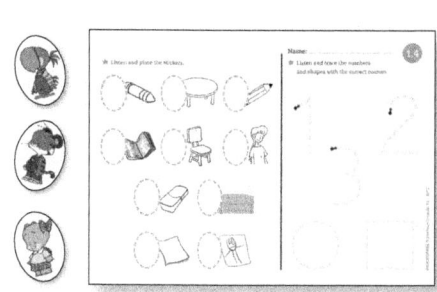

Step-by-step

Lesson 5 A — Authentic song

Opening routine
The children wake up Tommy and sing together. The chosen songs are already known by the children and they may even remember some of the words.

Playing with Tommy
Introduce the vocabulary for the Authentic song by means of actions, sounds and mime so that the children become familiar with the concepts and situation that is going to be presented in the song.

Authentic song
The children listen to a traditional song in English, accompanied by gestures and interpretations. This is a fun way to introduce new vocabulary, as well as getting to know songs that form part of the oral tradition in the Anglo-Saxon world.

Worksheet
Activities that introduce the new vocabulary related to the song.

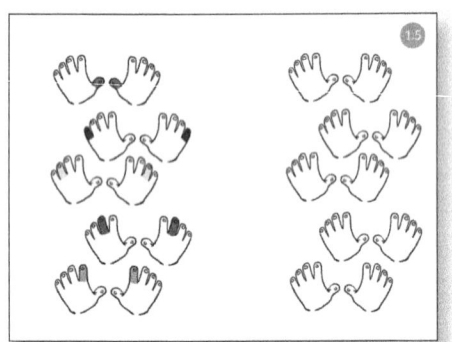
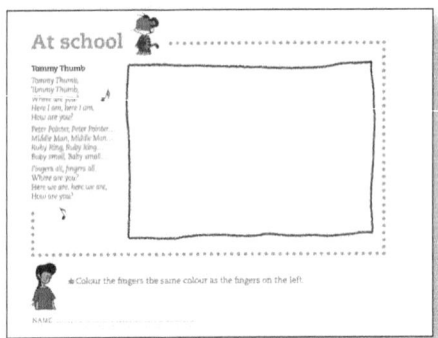
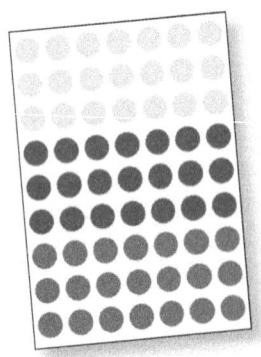

Lesson 5 B

This lesson is intended for those teachers who give more hours of class or for those who want to practise the vocabulary, expressions or the song in another way.

Authentic song
An opportunity to sing the traditional song, this time in a more active way so that the children can now try to follow the words and relate the story that the song tells, with mime and actions.

Photocopiable worksheet
This photocopiable worksheet shows a template related to the Authentic song that can be used to create a Very Big Class Song Book.

Step-by-step

Lesson 6 A  Photo poster

Opening routine
The children wake up Polly and sing together. They can go over the Authentic song seen in the previous lesson or another song suggested on the list, one that the children already know and can sing together without difficulty.

Photo poster
The poster offers the children images of objects and real situations to broaden their vocabulary and knowledge. With audio help, this activity is perfect for applying what has been learnt to a practical context.

Worksheet
Using the worksheet and the stickers, the children learn new vocabulary related to the photo poster. The marks where the stickers should be stuck are not normally shown on the children's copy of the worksheet, so that the children have to think about where they need to stick them or refer to the teacher's worksheet. This activity helps them to develop logical dexterity.

 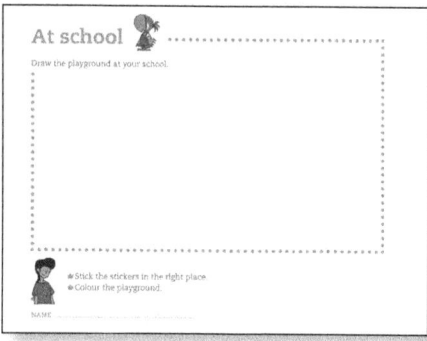 

Lesson 6 B

In this last lesson, the children revise the vocabulary and concepts learnt in Lesson A using mime, games and flashcards, participating in a fun way.

Photo poster
Using the posters as a visual reference and through games, this activity is an opportunity to revise the vocabulary and concepts learnt in the lesson and to apply them to real world images.

Photocopiable worksheet
This photocopiable worksheet shows a drawing related to the activities in this lesson so that the children can revise the vocabulary and colour the worksheet. This activity is a perfect opportunity to observe if the children have understood and assimilated the vocabulary and concepts from Lesson A.

Basic Competences

Key Competences

The Organic Education Law incorporates eight Basic Competences into the curriculum from Primary Education onwards. They are knowledge, skills and attitudes that everyone needs for their school career, their personal development and their inclusion in society. They are acquired and improved upon throughout the different stages of education.

By including the Basic Competences in *Big Jungle Fun* we are trying to encourage the initial development of these competences. Throughout this course, the children work on **competence in linguistic communication** which contributes towards the development and acquisition of the English language: it allows the children to express themselves and to understand simple messages.
It also serves as an introduction to the other key competences that the children need to cope in today's society. The competences form the base of a continual learning process throughout their lives.

Units	1	2	3	4	5	6	7	8	9
Autonomy and personal initiative				●	●	●	●	●	●
Mathematical competence	●	●		●	●		●	●	
Social competence and citizenship	●	●	●		●	●		●	
Knowledge and interaction with the physical world		●	●	●	●	●	●	●	●
Digital competence			●			●			
Learning to learn	●			●					●
Cultural and artistic competence	●	●			●		●	●	

Basic Competences

Mathematical competence

Initiation in key mathematical skills. The children practise the correct linguistic expression and way of writing the numbers and have the opportunity to count objects and recognize written numbers. They start to acquire a logical way of thinking in order to solve everyday problems.

Knowledge and interaction with the physical world

There are a series of exercises related to people, objects and other elements of the world around us. The physical world that the child is beginning to discover and the new knowledge that they will be acquiring, will allow them to better understand the elements of nature and the relationships that human beings maintain with their environment.

Digital competence

This area provides skills for finding, selecting and understanding information. The children familiarise themselves with how new technology operates and how to use it in the English class.

Social competence and citizenship

The children learn to communicate with others, to understand what others are conveying to them and other skills necessary for coexistence. The child's socialisation begins: they have to share, follow certain rules, learn social traditions and so on.

Cultural and artistic competence

In this method there are many opportunities to develop a cultural and artistic education through the stories, songs and art activities. Also, acting out the parts of the story characters through mime will help the children to develop their creative and expressive abilities.

Learning to learn

Activities that work on attention, memory or construction of meaning serve to contribute towards the development of learning.
This competence helps develop and integrate new learning and improve the capacity to learn independently.

Autonomy and personal initiative

Those activities that oblige the children to put themselves in someone else's place, make decisions or decide between various issues, promote the development of this competency. It allows the children to act on their own initiative and encourages the process of self-esteem.

Some advice

1. You and the class teacher

- **Organisation and rules in the class**
  The teacher will show the children how to work together and organize themselves in small groups and individually. It would be helpful to know how the teacher does this and follow his or her example to establish some class routines:
  – To give out and collect the crayons and books.
  – For when a child wants to drink water or go to the toilet.
  – To know how the children enter the classroom and sit in a circle.
  – To know what to do if the children get rowdy (relaxation techniques).
  – To establish acceptable limits of behavior and know what to do when the children overstep them.

  The class teacher may also tell you about what the children are like and the factors that may affect their behavior and learning.

- **Become a familiar part of their day**
  The fact that the children see a fluid communication between their teacher and you helps a lot. It is, therefore, useful if you spend some time before starting the classes with the teacher, helping them and observing.
  Then encourage the children to sing and show the teacher the work that they have been doing with you in class.

- **Basic concepts and art and craft activities**
  It will also be necessary to co-ordinate with the teacher what the basic concepts constitute so that there is continuity in the development of the subject matter being taught in the mother tongue and their learning in English. This helps to consolidate concepts and find out if the children are having any problems. Also check if you can use classroom materials for art and craft activities.

2. How to involve the children's families

At this age the family is the main point of reference for the children. The ties between school and home shown in *Big Jungle Fun* are the following:
– In each unit, the children have a pop-out that they take home to show their parents and use to sing the song and tell them the story.
– On the Multi-ROM are a selection of songs which the children can listen to, act out or sing at home or in the car. They also have the student's version of the traditional stories and computer games to reinforce the content of each unit.
– At the beginning of each term, a letter is sent to the parents informing them of the vocabulary and songs that the children are going to learn and to give them ideas about how to reinforce what is being taught outside school. There is an evaluation sheet at the end of each term so that the children can show their parents what they have learnt, what they found most difficult and what they do best. When possible, you can make a video or a DVD of the children singing the songs and acting out the stories and send it to the parents.

You could make a *Big Jungle Fun* book with photographs of the English class and send it to the parents. At Christmas and in the summer, you can invite the parents to the class to see a show of the songs and stories that the children have learnt.

Some advice

3. How to use the *Big Jungle Fun* puppets

Tommy and Tina are soft toy animals and Polly is a puppet and a soft toy too. They are funny, playful very good-natured and they love to play!

You can use Tommy, Tina and Polly in the following ways:
- At the beginning of the class, the children can wake up one or all of the characters by saying their name (not too loudly, so they don't get a fright).
- As a routine marker: to begin a table activity, for example, the characters can ask the children to sit down.
- At the end of the class. The children can sing and say goodbye to the characters.
- To teach new words or explain a game. The characters can whisper in your ear so that you can tell the children what they have told you.
- As part of a game. Fantasy forms an essential part of children's lives, therefore a game can be much more fun if it is Tina, Tommy and Polly who are playing it in your place. For example, Tommy can show the children what they have to do, he can choose who is going to be the player and he can be the one to say: Very good!
- Tommy and his friends only speak English, therefore although you sometimes use your mother tongue, they can't speak any language that isn't English.
- You can take photographs of the toys with different objects, in different places or doing various activities in order to coincide with the themes in each unit.

4. English versus the children's mother tongue

The more English that the children hear the better, as it is essential that they understand that English is a language and, therefore, a means of communication. Also, children of this age are good at guessing or intuiting meaning, as they are accustomed to not understanding many of the words in their mother tongue.
Using lots of mime and an expressive intonation will allow you to use far more English than you may have thought possible.
Inevitably, the children will habitually use their mother tongue; a very useful strategy is to respond to their contributions with enthusiasm and then paraphrase what they said in English. In the guide you will find various descriptions, explorations and questions that the teacher can find helpful to use in different situations and in English.
Summing up: remember that it is best to start talking a little in the children's mother tongue and to finish talking in English. Not the other way around!

5. How to play *Guess the magic word*

Bring Tommy into class in a bag and explain that he's sleeping. Explain that to wake him up, children will have to guess the magic word. Give the children a clue as to what the word might be: *I think the magic word is something in the classroom.* Children say words to try to wake Tommy up. After each try, look into the bag and say: *No, (crayon) isn't the magic word! Tommy's still sleeping!* After several attempts, say: *Yes! (pencil) was the magic word. Here's Tommy!*

Big Book

In the *Big Jungle Fun* Big Book the course's three main characters star in four new adventures. With these fantastic stories you can practise the vocabulary and concepts which helps to improve the children's learning experience. The Big Book is a resource that the teacher can use whenever necessary and for whatever purpose they want: for fun or as a teaching aid that serves as a general reinforcement of the acquired knowledge. The drawings can be used in question and answer sessions, for example: *What can you see here? What colour is (the bird)? How many (lions) are there? Where is (Tommy)? Come and point to the (circle).*

❋ Tommy and Tina's race
This is a version of the fable "The Hare and the Tortoise". In the story Tommy is faster than Tina, but he is easily distracted whilst Tina is slow but sure and steady, so she follows the race with determination towards victory. During the story, the numbers up to ten, toys and animals are revised. There are butterflies on all the pages: ask the children to count them as you read the story.

❋ Animal colours
This story revises animals, colours and classroom vocabulary. The drawings of the colours that the children know from the flashcards come to life with the help of Twig and Petal. The children will enjoy imitating the animal noises and singing the colour songs.

❋ Hunt the shapes
This story revises animals, geometric shapes and the natural world; the teacher hides the shapes and the three friends have fun searching for them.

❋ I want my favourite teddy!
This story deals with Twig's baby brother; the family helps the baby to find his favourite teddy all over the house without success. Prepositions, the colours, the family, furniture and clothes are all practised.

The Jungle Fun cube

The **Jungle Fun cube** is an inflatable die with a transparent pocket on each face to put flashcards in.

OBJECTIVES

The aim of using the die in the class is to:
- Help assimilate different concepts through play.
- Develop the imagination by creating new games.
- Improve social abilities through team games or by making each child wait their turn.
- Help with motor skills and coordination.
- Reinforce vocabulary that has been learnt.

SUGGESTED ACTIVITIES

- Identify as a group the concepts or vocabulary represented on the cards.
- You can give the class *carte blanche*, make teams or play individually.
- You can put the number flashcards in the pockets and use it as you would a normal die, or place other flashcards in the pockets, roll the die and …

  - Get as many things as the number indicated on the flashcard. Jump/clap/step as many times as the number indicates.

  - Collect classroom objects of the same colour as the flashcard indicated.

  - Name the object shown on the flashcard when you have thrown the die.

  - Put each character in a different pocket. Hide a flashcard behind the characters and ask the children which corresponds to each character: for example: *Where is red? With Tina.*

  - Use the die to show the flashcards from the unit.

  - Toss the die to decide who starts a game, who sings a song, who chooses the story, who gives out the worksheets … for example, you could place members of the family in the die, name one of them and make the children throw the die. The first pupil who throws the die and gets the family member that you named, wins.

  - Draw trails on the classroom floor or in the playground: a giant snakes and ladders, ludo, etc. and use the die for the throws.

  - Divide the class into two teams and ask each one to choose a word that is on the die. The children throw the die to see whose word comes up first.

  - Ask a group to move away so that they cannot see the die and throw it for the rest of the class to see. The group approaches and has to guess the word from the mimes of the rest of the class.

  - As in the game above, but in this case the group of children guessing have to ask questions to which the others may answer *yes* or *no*.

  - Place six flashcards in the die and show them to the class. One of the children chooses a card in secret and the rest try to guess which one. When they do, the child shows them that side of the die.

  - Throw the die into the air. Before it falls to the floor encourage the children to guess on which side it will fall.

Games

Once the children are familiar with the routine of the English class it is important that you do something completely different every now and then and surprise them as a way of getting their attention.

Here you have a list of games for those occasions. Many of them require a bit more time and are more active than the games suggested in the teachers' guide; in fact, some of them are best played in a gym or at playtime.

1. **Pass the parcel**
   Put an object or flashcard into a bag without the children seeing what it is. Play music as they pass the bag to one another. When you stop the music, the child holding the bag opens it and shows the object or flashcard to the others who say the name of the object. You can also play *Pass the parcel* with the children trying to guess the word before the bag is opened.

2. **Circle game**
   Form a circle with the whole class and ask one child to go in the middle. Show the children a small object, such as a toy car, which they then pass, unseen, behind their backs. The child in the middle says the name of another child and the object, for example: *Tomás (have you got the) car?* The others answer *No* until the child guesses correctly. Then they change places. You can play this game to the rhythm of the music: whilst the music plays, the children pass the object and when the music stops, they stop too. The child that is in the middle has a limited time (for example, 15 seconds) to guess who has the object before the music starts again. It can be played with more than one object.

3. **Chinese whispers**
   Place all the flashcards on the floor in front of the class. The children make two lines. Whisper a word to the children at the back of the lines, they then whisper the word to the next child until it reaches the children at the front of the lines. They then have to choose the correct flashcard and hand it in. This game can be made more competitive by whispering the same word to each group.

4. **Flashcard race**
   Place all the flashcards on the floor in front of the class. Draw a line at the back of the class and ask two children to stand behind the line. Say their name and a flashcard to each one and they have to find it and hand it to you. For example: *María find the apple/ José find the jacket. One, two, three, go!* This is not necessarily a race, you need to make this clear and encourage both children: *Very good.*

5. **Are you hungry, Mr Wolf?**
   Photocopy various food flashcards (you could also bring plastic food to the class). There should be the same number of flashcards or pieces of food as children and each food is repeated. Give each child a flashcard or piece of food. They make a line behind you and stand with their backs to the wall. You be the wolf. Ask them to repeat with you: *Are you hungry, Mr Wolf?* Start walking so that the children walk behind you. They ask: *Are you hungry, Mr Wolf?* over and over. You answer: *No.* After they have asked several times, answer: *Yes, and I want to eat a pear.* Try to catch all the children who have a pear whilst they run back to the start of the game. If they get back before you have caught them, then the wolf doesn't eat the pear!

Games

6. Ball in the bucket
Prepare some buckets or other containers before starting the class. You can practise the numbers, colours or flashcard words by putting the information on the buckets.
You will also need some soft balls.
Draw a line on the floor (the distance between the line and the buckets depends on the age of the children). The child or children stand behind the line with their ball. After saying for example, *three*, whoever has the ball tries to get it into the bucket marked 3.

7. Skittles
This is similar to the previous game. Make six skittles using the rolls from inside kitchen paper or plastic bottles. Write a number on each skittle to practise the numbers or write what you want to revise on a piece of paper and stick it near the skittle. For the colours, simply stick a piece of coloured paper on each skittle.
You will need some soft balls.
Place the skittles upright in the shape of a triangle. Draw a line on the floor. Ask a child to stand behind the line and roll a ball. They have to knock over as many skittles as they can. To give them more goes you can use 1, 2 or 3 balls. The children should say the word that corresponds to the skittle they have knocked over.

8. Swap
The children sit in a circle. When you say *Everyone wearing red swap … Now!* The children wearing something red change places. Whilst this is happening everyone says *Red red red*. You can practise vocabulary with this game by giving the children objects and flashcards and using all the words that you want them to learn: *Everyone with a toy/an animal/ clothes/ swap … Now!*

9. Mr Crocodile and the river
Draw a river on the classroom floor.
Tell the children that you are a crocodile and that you are very hungry.
Say: *Everyone wearing yellow can cross my river.* The children wearing yellow can cross the river. When they are on the other side, the others have to cross the river whilst trying not to get caught. Then choose a child to be the crocodile.
You can also practise vocabulary by giving the children flashcards. Say: *Everyone with (an animal) can cross my river.* Everyone that has an animal flashcard says the name of the animal or makes its noise and can then cross the river. Everyone else tries to cross without the crocodile catching them.

10. Hunt
Place all the flashcards on the floor.
Divide the children into flashcard categories and

ask each one of them to hunt the flashcards that correspond to them. You can also ask each child to hunt the flashcards that you tell them to. After five minutes, call them into the middle and ask them to name and show to the class the cards that they have found.

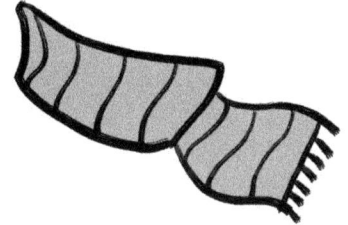

Celebrations

These six optional worksheets, are creative activities for the English class. The instructions suggest ways to use the worksheets; each teacher can make the activities as creative and innovative as they wish, using glitter, stickers and other materials.

You should co-ordinate these ideas with the class teacher so that the classes complement each other rather than overlap.
It is good to use as much English as possible to give instructions and to talk about what the children are doing or what is going on around them.

Autumn page 135
Show the children the hedgehog and ask them to colour it. Give them some scissors and glue so that they can cut out and glue the drawing onto cardboard. Give them also some brown card for them to cut and glue more spines on the hedgehog.

Halloween page 136
Show the class the cat mask and ask them to colour it black. Give them the card to glue the mask on it, and then cut it out. Help them to cut the eyes out and put an elastic band or a straw on it.

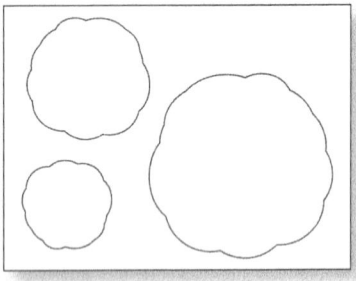

Winter page 137
Show the children the shapes in the worksheet. Ask them to cut the pieces out and to glue them onto a dark piece of card to make a snowman. Then ask them to draw and colour the details: scarf, buttons, arms and face.

Spring page 138
Show the picture of spring and explain that they are going to do a puzzle. Ask them to colour the scene and, once they have finished, to glue it onto cardboard. Show them how to draw several vertical and horizontal lines on the back to make the pieces. The children cut along the lines and then try to make their puzzle.

Easter page 139
Show the class the drawing with the basket and the Easter eggs. Give them crayons or colouring pencils for them to colour them. Help them to cut the eggs out and glue them on the basket.

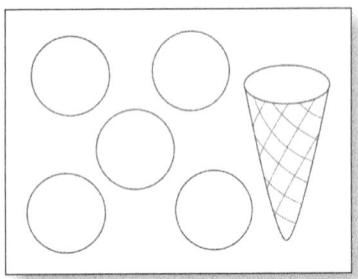

Summer page 140
Show the children the cone and the ice cream balls. Ask them to colour them. Then, they cut out the pieces and glue them onto cardboard to make a big ice cream.

Starter activities

Reviewing/Introducing Tommy, Tina and Polly

* Show Tommy, Tina and Polly to the children. For classes who haven't been introduced to them before, you can reveal them bit by bit so the children can guess that they are a tiger, a tortoise and a parrot.

Introducing Tommy to the children

* For classes that haven't been introduced to the characters, go around the circle with them saying: *Hello. My name's (Tommy). What's your name?* The children answer and give him a hug. For classes who already know the characters, ask them if they remember their names, or any story or song from the previous year. For example: *Are you feeling sleepy today?*

Singing a song or doing an action chant with Tommy, Tina and Polly

* Sing **Hello!** **1.1** saying the name of one of the children in each pause in the song. Every time you say a name, take Tommy over to the child so they can give him a kiss. With classes who already know Tommy you can pass him to a child for them to give him a hug and then they pass him on to the next child. Continue in turn around the whole group.
* Do **Tina's gym** **1.7** with the children standing in a circle.
* Sing **The weather song** **1.8** and **The days of the week** **1.9**.

Doing a drawing for Tommy

* The children do a drawing of their holidays for Tommy and he goes around the class asking them: *Tell me about your picture. What/who's that?* Translate their replies into English so Tommy can understand what the children say and make comments.

Flashcard games
to be used with the Teacher's Book

(in alphabetical order)

* **Bring me...**
Put all the unit flashcards on the floor. Ask a child to choose a flashcard, name it and give it to Tommy. Continue until there are no flashcards left.

* **Clever parrots**
Show the flashcards one by one and name them. Ask the children what parrots do (repeat). Explain to them that they are going to be intelligent parrots and, therefore, they are only going to repeat when the word you say matches the picture on the flashcard. Say one word repeatedly and show the flashcards one by one. The children keep quiet. When the flashcard that corresponds with your word is shown, they repeat it.

* **Descriptions game**
Put all the flashcards where the children can see them. Choose an item of clothing in secret. Invent sentences around the item of clothing

Flashcard games

for the children to guess what you are talking about: *You wear this when it is cold. You wear this on your head. It is yellow.*

Disappearing cards
Put all the flashcards in a line on the floor. The children name them in order. When they can do this easily, turn the flashcards over so that the children have to remember the words in order.

Echo
Say one of the words aloud and the children repeat it three times, each time a little quieter.

Fast and slow repeating game
Show the flashcards and name them quickly or slowly. The children repeat them in the same way.

Flash
Show a flashcard very quickly and then more slowly, until the children say what they can see.

Flashcard race
Put the flashcards on the floor in three groups. Call out three children and give them Tommy, Tina and Polly. Say, for example: *Tommy find yellow, Tina find the sofa, Polly find daddy*. The children take their character to help them find the corresponding flashcard and give it to you.

Guessing game
Put the flashcards on the carpet or the blackboard for the children to name them. Choose an animal. Make gestures mimicking the animal and say sentences for the children to guess what it is: *It has four legs. It's big. It's black and white or brown. It says moo*. After every sentence help them to rule out animals.

Guess my card
Show the flashcards to the children for them to name. Tommy chooses a flashcard and hides it from the children. The children take turns trying to guess the word. The child that guesses correctly takes Tommy's place.

Help the teacher
Hold the flashcards above your head in a pile as if they were a pack of cards, so that the children can see the first one but you can't. Name the words one by one; the children reply *Yes* or *No* depending on whether you name the word that corresponds to the picture.

Jump
Say one word repeatedly (*cheese*), at the same time showing the children the flashcards one by one. When you get to the *cheese* flashcard, they jump. Repeat with other words.

Keyhole
Draw and cut out a keyhole (approximately 5 cm long and 3 cm wide) in the centre of an A4 piece of card. Put a flashcard behind the keyhole and move it in a way that the children can see different parts of the drawing until they are able to identify it and name the corresponding word.

Memory
Show the children several flashcards and then hold the cards fanned out in a way that you can see them, but the children can't. The aim of the game is for the children to remember all the words. Every time a child says one of the words, put the corresponding flashcard face up on the table.

Miming flashcards
Show the flashcards and establish a mimicking gesture for each one. Choose one and do the gesture. The children name it. Once you have practised the game for a little while, the children can take on your role.

Move please, Tommy
Put a flashcard on the floor with Tommy partially hiding the picture. Say: *Can you move please, Tommy?* Move Tommy away from the flashcard little by little and ask: *What is it? Is it a…? Is it a…? Oh! It's a…!* Encourage the children to participate.

Moving cards
Show the flashcards and then put them face down. Mix them up and then point to one. The children help the characters to say the word, turn it over to see if they are correct.

Flashcard games

✤ Partial reveal
Cover a flashcard with a piece of paper. Move it slowly up, down, left or right and discover the image bit by bit until the children name the word that corresponds to the flashcard.

✤ Same or different?
Put the flashcards face down on the floor. Call out a child to put a school object on one of the flashcards. The child helps Tommy to turn it over. If the flashcard corresponds with the object, Tommy puts it to one side. If not, the child will put the flashcard face up again on the floor.

✤ Say it like me
Tommy says the words: *brother, sister, grandad, mummy, daddy, baby, granny, sofa, bed, bath* in different ways, for example, sometimes in a loud voice, sometimes in a quiet voice or sometimes fast and sometimes slowly. The children repeat the words Tommy says, imitating the way he says them.

✤ Stop
Place the cards upside down and ask a child to choose one and show it to the class. The whole class says the word out loud. Place the flashcard back in the deck and shuffle it. Turn the cards around one by one; the children must say *Stop!* when they see that one flashcard.

✤ Tommy guesses game
Put the objects or the flashcards on the floor. Call out a child to choose a flashcard. Tommy covers his eyes with his paws whilst the child chooses. Then, Tommy uncovers his eyes and tries to guess which flashcard the child has chosen. You can cover and uncover your eyes at the same time as Tommy. Say: *Come here, (Marisa). Close your eyes, Tommy. Choose one, (Marisa). Show it to the class. Put it back. Open your eyes, Tommy.* In Tommy's voice, ask: *Is it the…?*

✤ Tommy's instructions
Call out several children. Tommy says: *Give the (crayon) to the teacher, please. Put the (crayon) on the chair, please.* Help the children to carry out the instructions as necessary.

✤ Walk to the…
Go over some actions with the children. Say: *walk, hop, tiptoe, jump* and the children do the corresponding actions. Put the flashcards on different walls of the classroom. Name two or three children and say: (*Walk to teddy*). Repeat with different children, actions and flashcards.

✤ Watch my lips
Tommy whispers one of the words to you. Mouth the word without making any noise. The children watch your lips and say the word. Tommy says: *Well done!*

✤ What does Tommy have?
Put three flashcards on the carpet, face up, and sit Tommy, Tina and Polly on top of them. Ask the children: *What toy does (Polly) have?* When they have guessed the three flashcards, repeat with other toys.

✤ What's missing?
Put four flashcards on the carpet. The children name them. Take away the flashcards and this time only put down three. The children name the flashcard that is missing. Play again with different flashcards.

✤ What's Tommy sitting on?
Put three flashcards face up on the floor and sit the three characters on top of them. The children guess what each character is sitting on. Say: *What's (Tommy) sitting on? Yes! It's the (picture). / No! What's this?*

✤ Where are they?
Show the children the flashcards for them to name them. Choose three family members and put them underneath the furniture flashcards. Ask: *Who is in the bath/ on the sofa/ in bed?* Repeat with other family members.

✤ Which one?
Put the flashcards face down on the floor. Say: *Where's the (pencil)?* Call out a child and give him/ her Tommy to hold. He/ she helps him to look for the pencil, turning over the flashcards one by one. Say: *No. That isn't the (pencil)! It's the… Yes! Here's the (pencil)! Well done!*

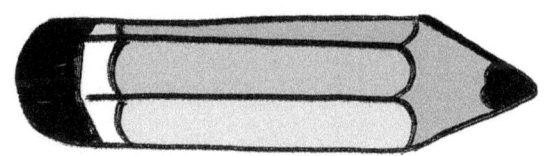

Big Book of traditional stories

This beautiful Story Book contains three popular stories from the Anglo-Saxon world that will also be known to the children in their own language. The stories have been carefully adapted and edited to aid the practice of the vocabulary and concepts contained in *Big Jungle Fun*. Each story corresponds to a school term.

* **Goldilocks and the three bears**

In this well-known story the little girl goes into the three bears' house and tries the food, the chairs and the beds. They all have a big surprise when the bears come home!

This story revises the vocabulary in units 1 and 2.

* **The king and the magic clothes**

This is an adaptation of the famous story about a very vain king and the tailors who tricked him into buying expensive but invisible clothes.

This story revises the vocabulary from units 4, 5 and 6.

* **The three Billy Goats**

The three brothers dream of crossing the river to get to the delicious green grass on the other side. Unfortunately, in order to do this, they must face the monster who lives below the bridge.

This story revises the vocabulary in units 7, 8 and 9.

Goldilocks and the three bears

Name:

Goldilocks and the three bears

VOCABULARY AND LANGUAGE

table, chair, bed
mummy, daddy, baby, granny, grandad, brother, sister
kitchen, living room, bedroom, stairs
walk, house, door, bowl, soup
yellow, pink, green, orange
enormous, big, little
go, see, eat, break, go to sleep, come home, jump, run
up, down, into, out of
Goldilocks tries the soup / the enormous chair /
the enormous bed.
It's too hot / cold / big / hard / soft / just right.
Yummy yummy! Ouch! Ugh!
I like soup!
I'm sleepy.
Someone's been eating my soup!
Someone's been sitting in my chair!
Someone's been sleeping in my bed!
It's all finished!
It's broken!
She's still here!

AUDIOS

Traditional story: Goldilocks and the three bears 1

Story song: The three bears 2

Three brown bears, (x2)
Very grumpy bears. (x2)
Someone's been eating my soup!
Mine too! Mine too!
And we don't know who!

Three brown bears, (x2)
Very grumpy bears. (x2)
Someone's been sitting in my chair!
Mine too! Mine too!
And we don't know who!

Three brown bears, (x2)
Very grumpy bears. (x2)
Someone's been sleeping in my bed!
Mine too!
And now we know who!

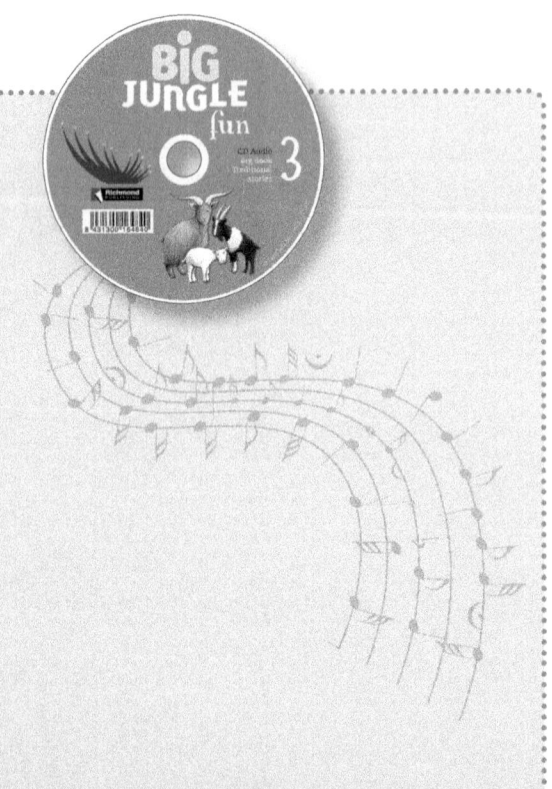

Goldilocks and the three bears

Story music 3

You're Goldilocks going into the bears' house. Stop.
Eat the soup. Stop.
Sit on the chairs. Stop.
Jump on the beds. Stop.
You're sleepy. Go to sleep. Stop.
Yipes! There's a bear! Jump out of bed and run across the room. Stop.
Run down the stairs. Stop.
And out of the door. Stop.
Phew... Safe!

Songs to revise:

I can paint a picture	1.22
Where's mummy?	1.27
Do you know your numbers?	1.13
Tommy thumb	3.1
Five little ducks	3.4
Tina´s gym	1.7

Traditional story: *Goldilocks and the three bears*: Student´s version 4

MATERIALS

- Flashcards: *table, chair, mummy, daddy, baby, sofa, bed, bath, little, big, circle, triangle, square*
- Big Jungle Flashcards: *soup, garden, eat, jump, run, grumpy, sleepy, kitchen, living room, bedroom, stairs*
- A bowl and a spoon (Presentation of the story)
- An arrow or a baby bear made from stiff card. If you decide to use a baby bear photocopy, stick onto card and cut out the baby bear from page 8 of the story (While reading activities).
- Big Book and flashcard for *grumpy* (Story song)
- Flashcards: *kitchen, living room, bedroom, stairs* and *garden*. Three bowls of different sizes and three spoons, three chairs of different sizes and three mats the younger children use for their afternoon naps (Acting out the story)
- Large piece of card (**A letter to the bears**)
- Photos of different bears (two brown bears, two polar bears, two pandas, a brown bear with one or two cubs, a brown bear standing, using it's claws to eat berries, running on all fours, a brown bear fishing) downloaded from the internet or cut out from magazines. (Cross curricular activities: **Investigating bears**.)
- A *Save the Bears* badge for each child. These can be round pieces of card with the text written on them but with plenty of space for the children to draw their bears. A completed *Save the Bears* badge to show them, with a strip of stick-on Velcro on the back. You can put the other side of the Velcro on your shirt or jacket. Scissors, crayons, a roll of stick-on Velcro. (Cross curricular activities: **Making a Save the Bears badge**)
- Pictures of things that are hot and cold, for example: a summer's day, a pot of soup, a fire, a snowman, an ice-cream, an icicle. (Cross curricular: **Hot and cold**)
- A large house drawn on continuous paper, card, Blu tack, tape, a photocopy of the three bears and Goldilocks. (Art and craft activities: **Making a poster story**)

Goldilocks and the three bears

Presentation of the story

- Show the children the flashcard of *soup* and the bowl and spoon. Mime smelling the contents and say: *Yummy, yummy! I like soup!* Mime tasting a bit and say: *Ouch! Too hot! / Ugh! Too cold! / Yummy! Just right!* The children can come out to mime trying the soup. Ask them: *Is it too hot, too cold or just right?* Say: *Today's story has three bowls of soup!*
- **Introduce the story:** Show the children the first page. Point and say: *Here is a little girl. Her name is Goldilocks* (you can explain it is because of the colour of her hair). *She is going for a walk in the wood. Look at the little house! The door is open. Do you think Goldilocks goes inside?* Repeat the children's predictions in English.

While listening activities

First reading

You can go through the story commenting and asking children to predict what happens, repeating what they say in English, until you get to page 10. Ask the children what they think the bears are going to say about the soup and the broken chair. Tell them you are going to listen to the story to find out what the ending is. Play the story on the audio. Alternatively, play the audio and show the pages one by one, pausing to ask questions. Point to the characters and mime to help comprehension. Repeat children's answers in English as necessary.

QUESTIONS:

Pages 2, 4, 6:	What does Goldilocks see? Do you think she tries the soup / the chairs / the beds?
Page 4:	Does she like this soup? And this soup? What does she do?
Page 6:	Does she like this chair? And this chair? What does she do?
Page 8:	Does she like this bed? And this bed? What does she do?
Page 9:	Who lives in the house?
Pages 10, 11 and 12:	What do the bears say? Are they happy?
Page 13:	What does Goldilocks do?
Page 14:	Does Goldilocks go back to the house? What does she say in the letter on the table?

Goldilocks and the three bears

Subsequent readings

- Call a child out to help you turn the pages.
- Teach children a mime for *enormous*, *big* and *little*. Tell them to listen and do the mimes every time they hear the words.
- Show a page and call children out to stick the story arrow / baby bear on: *Goldilocks, the house, the door, the soup that is too (hot) / just right, the (enormous) chair, the bed that is too (hard) / just right, (Daddy) Bear* before you read the page.
- Put the flashcards: *chair, sofa, bed, bath, picture, table, crayon, paper, pencil* on the carpet / board. Before you read each page ask children to look and see if any of the objects on the flashcards are on the page. Remove them as children see them (the only ones that aren't there are *sofa* and *bath*).
- Encourage the children to join in with the actions of the story and with some of the lines: *Ouch! Too hot / Ugh! Too cold! Oh no! Too big! / Just right! Ouch too hard! / Oh no! Too soft! / Just right! Someone's been (eating my soup)*. You can use Polly for this. First Polly imitates the characters and their voices and then the children join in saying it again. You can make this into a chant, for example, Polly says a line in a rhythmic fashion, the children repeat it:

> (Polly) *Someone has*
> (children) *Someone has*
> (Polly) *been eating*
> (children) *been eating*
> (Polly) *my soup!*
> (children) *my soup!*
> continue with *Someone has been sitting in my chair / sleeping in my bed.*

- Before the class, cover some of the characters and objects with post its. As you read the story the children say who or what is behind the post its.
- Say a sentence from the story and turn the pages. The children say *Stop* when you get to the appropriate page.
- Tell the story making mistakes for the children to correct, for example, page 1: *The door is closed. (No! The door is open)*. Page 2: *Goldilocks goes into the bathroom. (No! The kitchen)*. You can use Tommy to do this activity.

After listening activities

- Story song: *The three bears song* 2 You need the Big Book and the flashcard for *grumpy*.
- Show page 9. Ask the children how the bears feel and show them the flashcard for *grumpy*. Remember with the children mimes for *bear, grumpy, Someone's been eating my soup! Mine too* and *We don't know who!* Say the first verse encouraging the children to join in with the mimes. Repeat with page 10 *Someone's been sitting in my chair* and page 11 *Someone's been sleeping in my bed. And now we know who.*
- Play the song on the CD and encourage the children to join in the mimes with you. Show pages 9, 10 and 11 out of order and sing the appropriate verses with the children.
- If the children have already made their bear puppets, they can hold these up as they sing the song. You can also call three children out to be the bears. They lead the rest of the class saying and singing their lines.
- Sing the song pausing for the children to sing the next word(s) for example: *Three brown… Someone's been eating my…*
- Sing the song but make mistakes, for example: *Four brown bears. Someone's been sleeping in my soup.* The children correct you.

Acting out the characters

- Look through the book with the children and ask them to tell you the characters (Goldilocks, Daddy, Mummy and Baby Bear). Mime looking in a bowl in a surprised way, upturning it and then bursting into tears. Ask the children: *Who am I?* Continue with the other characters. Children can volunteer to take over your role. They whisper to you before acting out the character so you can help them!

Story Pictionary

- Start drawing something that is in the story (house, stairs, little bear, bowl, chair, bed…). Children guess what it is, name it and find a page in the book where it appears.

Goldilocks and the three bears

Activities to practise the vocabulary from the story

(1) **Using flashcards**

* **Flashcards:** *mummy, daddy, baby, table, chair, bed*
  - Show the *mummy, daddy* and *baby* flashcards. Draw three circles on the board and put a flashcard face down in each one. Ask the children to guess the family members. When they have guessed, show them the table, chair and bed flashcards and play a memory game. Put the family flashcards on the furniture flashcards and say: *(Mummy's on the bed, daddy's on the chair and baby's on the table).* Turn the flashcards over and ask: *Where's (mummy)?*
  - For more flashcard games see page 25.

* **Story flashcards** *kitchen, living room, bedroom, stairs, table, chair, bed, bath, picture*
  - Put the *kitchen, living room* and *bedroom* flashcards on the board / carpet. Name a child then mime and ask where Goldilocks says one of the following: *Too hot! / Too hard! / Too big! / Too cold! / Too soft! / Just right!* The child goes to the board and touches the relevant flashcard.
  - Put the room flashcards on the board and draw a bathroom. Using Tommy, pick up the bed flashcard and say: *The bed goes in the kitchen. No Tommy... Can you help Tommy, where does the bed go? Yes, in the bedroom.* Stick the bed flashcard beside the bedroom. Continue in the same way putting the *chair* with the *stairs* (then with the *living room*), the *table* with the *stairs* (then with the *kitchen*) and the *bath* with the *bedroom* (and then the *bathroom*). Ask what is left (*The picture*), and put it with the stairs. Ask children to close their eyes / look at the back of the classroom and mix the furniture up. They tell you in which rooms to put it. Ask questions like: *Where does the bed go? Yes, in the bedroom.*
  - For more flashcard games see page 25.

* **Vocabulary Worksheet S1.1**
  See **Presenting the worksheets** section on page 38.

---

(2) **Story music** ③ (you need the flashcards for *eat, run, jump, sleepy*)
Say: *You're Goldilocks going into the bears' house. / Eat the soup. / Sit on the chairs. / Jump on the beds. / You're sleepy. Go to sleep. / Yipes! There's a bear! Jump out of bed and run across the room. / Run down the stairs and out of the door. Phew... Safe!*

- Practise miming *eat, run, jump, sleepy* with the flashcards.
- Practise the actions without the music: Name children to come out and mime the actions of the story with you. Then all the children mime at the same time. To make this more fun say *Stop* and the children freeze between mimes.
- Play the story music and the children follow the instructions.

Goldilocks and the three bears

(3) **Story Worksheets S1.2 S1.3 S1.4**. See **Presenting the worksheets** section on page 38.
Note: The children should complete these worksheets before they do: Traditional story: *Goldilocks and the three bears*: Student´s version ④

- **Traditional story: *Goldilocks and the three bears*: Student´s version ④**
  - Listen to the audio: Children open their books and follow the story. Pause the CD to turn the page. Encourage the children to follow the story, to join in with the phrases they practised with Polly and to sing the song.
  - Games:

1
Say: *Where's Daddy Bear? 1, 2, 3.* The children look for the page in their books where there is a picture of Daddy Bear. Continue with words and phrases: *Goldilocks / Baby Bear / Mummy Bear / Someone's been sleeping in my bed! / Goldilocks tries the enormous chair. / Goldilocks tries the soup in the little bowl. Yummy! Just right!*

2
Flash a page of the book again and again, first very fast and then more slowly. Children say what they can see.

3
Choose a page. The children guess what is on it.

- **Acting out the story Worksheet S1.6** See Materials for what you need.
  - The children act out the story using: **Goldilocks and the three bears: Student´s version** ④:
  - The children press out their pencil puppets of the 3 bears and Goldilocks. **(Worksheet S3.6.)**. Help them to sellotape them to the ice-lolly sticks / straws / pencils.
  - Encourage them to hold up the characters as they listen to the story. Play the CD.
  - Call out children to play the part of Goldilocks, Daddy, Mummy and Baby Bear. Each of the characters brings the relevant pencil puppet.
  - Put the flashcards of the *kitchen, living room, bedroom, stairs* and *garden* going around the walls of the classroom. Put the three bowls and spoons in the kitchen, the three chairs in the living room and the three mats in the bedroom.
  - Read the part of the narrator and encourage the children to act out the story and to repeat expressions after you. Repeat with a different group of children.

- **A Letter to the three bears**

  Ask the children what they think about Goldilocks' behaviour. Remind them that she ate all Baby Bear's soup and broke his chair! Show them the letter of apology on page 13. Offer to write the letter they suggest. Begin *Dear Daddy, Mummy and Baby Bear,* and repeat in English what the children suggest. Write the letter on a large piece of card. Ask the children to draw, colour and cut out flowers to put around the letter. They can show the finished letter to their parents, other teachers and classes and tell them the story of Goldilocks.

Goldilocks and the three bears

Cross curricular activities

1. Investigating bears: Flashcards: *mountain, wood, river, tree, mummy, baby, eyes, nose, mouth, ears, legs, fish, apple, pear* and pictures of bears from magazines or downloaded from the internet (see Materials).

- Ask the children what they know about bears. Ask: *What colour are bears?* Show them the brown bear, the panda and the polar bear. Put the pairs of bears face down on the carpet and move them around. Play pelmanism. Call a child to turn two over and say the words. If the cards match say *Well done!* and take the cards out of the game. If they don't the child puts them face down in the same place and another child has a go. The class tries to remember where the cards are so they can make a pair.
- Ask the children if they have seen a brown bear in the zoo. What was it like? What was it doing? Ask what they would like to know about bears? Repeat what they say in English.

Talk about brown bears: Show the children the photos of bears and ask questions: *What colour are they? Can you point to the bear's eyes, ears, nose, mouth, legs and tail?*
  - Show the children the photos of how a bear can run on all four legs or use its front legs like arms and its claws like hands to pick fruit or catch fish. Ask: *Where do brown bears live? In woods and forests and on mountains. What do bears eat? Fruit, little animals and insects, honey and fish. How many babies do bears have? Between one and four.*
  - Ask them what bears do in the winter when it's cold and snowy. They sleep until it's warm and sunny.
  - Play games:
    1. Say: *You're bears. It's cold and cloudy and snowy. Go to sleep, little bears.* The children pretend to go to sleep. Say: *Wake up. It's spring and it's warm and sunny. Jump, little bears. Run, little bears. Eat, little bears.* The children follow your instructions until you say: *Oops... Here comes the snow! It's cold and cloudy and snowy. Go to sleep, little bears.*
    2. The children sit in a circle. One of the children is the bear and lies in a ball in the middle of the circle. The rest of the children chant with you: *Little bear, little bear sleeping in his cave. If someone goes to wake him, he'll growl and wave!* Make a sign to one of the children who creeps forward, touches the bear and goes back to their place. Say with the children: *Wake up little bear!* The bear guesses who touched him and growls and then waves to them.

- **Cross Curricular Worksheet S1.6.** See page 39.

Making a *Save the Bears* badge
  - Tell the children that in the past brown bears lived in all of Spain but now they only live in the north of Spain, in Asturias, Cantabria and Castilla León. You can show children on a map where these autonomous communities are or ask them if they have visited them.

Goldilocks and the three bears

- Tell children we need to look after them so they don't all disappear! There are only about 100 brown bears still living in the wild in Spain. Show the children the badge you have made and how to attach it to your shirt or jacket with the Velcro.
- Show them the badges you have prepared for them and say: *Draw a bear here.* You can draw the outline of a bear or a bear's head on the board for children to copy.
- As they finish their badges stick Velcro on the back and on their shirts / jumpers so they can wear them.

Teddy bear, teddy bear (Level 1)
- Say this chant from the Level 1 book: *Teddy bear, teddy bear, turn around. Teddy bear, teddy bear, touch the ground. Teddy bear, teddy bear, touch your nose. Teddy bear, teddy bear, touch your toes. Teddy bear, teddy bear, arms to the side. Teddy bear, teddy bear, arms out wide. Teddy bear, teddy bear, turn off the light. Teddy bear, teddy bear, say goodnight.*

2 Hot and cold:
(See Materials, page 31.)

- Show the children page 3 and ask what Goldilocks said: *Ouch! Too hot! Ugh! Too cold! Yummy! Just right!*
- Ask children if they remember eating something that was too hot. Repeat what they say in English. Ask if there is something they like that is cold and repeat what they say in English. Show them the photos you have downloaded from the internet and divide them into two piles. Encourage them to say: *It's hot* and *It's cold.*

Art and craft

1
Children can choose the scene they like best in the story and draw it. Go around and ask them what is happening in their pictures. Repeat what they say in English.

2
Children can make a **Poster Story.**
(See Materials, page 31)
Make three large windows out of card and stick one side of them to the house with tape so that they open. You can hold them closed with a piece of Blu tack. In the first window draw a table. Divide the children into three groups. One group draw and colour an enormous, a big and a little bowl to stick on the table. One group draw and colour an enormous, a big and a little chair to stick in the living room. One group draw and colour an enormous, a big and a little bed to stick in the bedroom. Supervise to check on the sizes or size the card that you give them to draw on or, alternatively, draw the objects yourself so they just colour them in. Trace or photocopy the bears and Goldilocks. Groups which finish early can colour the roof of the house or draw trees around it. The children can re-tell the story, moving Goldilocks and the bears from room to room, for other classes or their parents.

Goldilocks and the three bears

PRESENTING THE WORKSHEETS

* **Story Worksheet S1.1 (Sides A and B):** *Goldilocks, bowl, soup, table, chair, bed, enormous, big, little, red, blue, yellow*

    * **Revise** the colours and *table, chair, bed* with flashcard games.
    * **Display and talk about the worksheets:** Point and say: *Look! Here is Goldilocks and here is the house. Here is the (big) bowl. What does she say? Ouch, Too hot! Ugh, Too cold! Yummy, Just right! Look, she eats all the soup!* Show Side B of the worksheet and say: *Here is the (little) chair. Which one does Goldilocks sit on? Look, it's broken! Here's the (enormous) bed. Where's Goldilocks? Yes, she's sleeping in the little bed.*
    * **Practise the task.** Call out children and say: *Pick up a pencil and follow the lines on the roof. What colour are the bowls in the story? Pick up a (red) crayon and colour the bowl.*

    > **Table Time**
    >
    > * The children trace the lines on the roof of the house. They colour the bowls as in the story.
    > * Encourage the children to identify *Goldilocks, soup, table, chair, bed, enormous, big, little, red, blue, yellow.*

* **Story Worksheet S1.2 (Sides A and B):** *Daddy / Mummy / Baby Bear, someone's been eating my soup / sitting on my chair / sleeping in my bed, circle, triangle, square*

    * **Revise** *daddy, mummy, baby, circle, triangle, square* with flashcard games.
    * **Display and talk about the worksheets:** Point and say: *Who's this? Yes, it's (Daddy) Bear. They are coming to the house. Look at (Mummy) Bear. What is (she) saying?* Show Side B of the worksheet and say: *Look at (Baby) Bear. What is (he) saying?*
    * **Practise the task:** Call out children and say: *Pick up a crayon and finish colouring Goldilocks' hair. Good. Now look in this picture. Can you find the (circle)? Good. Get a pencil and follow the lines.*

    > **Table Time**
    >
    > * The children finish colouring Goldilocks' hair. They look for and trace the circle, triangle and square.
    > * Encourage the children to identify the bear family, the shapes and the lines from the story. If you have done *The three bears* song, sing it or play the CD while the children work.

* **Story Worksheet S1.3 (Sides A and B):** *Goldilocks, Mummy, Daddy, Baby Bear, bed, stairs, door, garden, circle, triangle, square, yellow, pink, green, orange*

    * **Revise**: *bed, stairs, door, garden, circle, triangle, pink, green, yellow, orange* with flashcard games.
    * **Display and talk about the worksheets:** Point and say: *Look! Here is Goldilocks. She jumps out of bed… runs across the bedroom, down the stairs and out of the door.* Show side B of the worksheet and say. *Look! Here is the bear family eating soup. Are they happy now?* Ask the children and show the last picture of the story in the Big Book if necessary.
    * **Practise the tasks:** Call children out. Say: *Look. Trace the lines on the stairs with your finger. Good. Now look on the back. Colour the soup. Thank you.*

Goldilocks and the three bears

> **Table Time**
> - The children trace the lines on the stairs and colour the soup.
> - Encourage the children to identify the characters, shapes, colours and *bedroom, stairs, door, garden*.
> - Sing the song or play it on the CD as the children are working and encourage them to join in.

Vocabulary Worksheet S1.4: *kitchen, living room, bedroom, stairs*

- **Display and talk about the worksheet:** Point to the pictures and ask the children questions. Ask: *Where do the bears go first? Good, to the kitchen to look at the bowls. Then where do they go? Good, to the living room to look at the chairs. Then where do they go? Good, to the bedroom to look at the beds. Then what happens? Good, Goldilocks goes running down the stairs... Here she is.*
- **Practise the tasks:** Call a child out. Point to the first picture and say: *Who is this? Where do they go next? Good.* Give the child some *gomets* and say: *Put the gomets in a line from the kitchen to the living room.* Continue with other children and pictures.

> **Table Time**
> - The children make *gomets* paths to show the order of the pictures from the story.
> - Encourage the children to say words in English about the pictures.

Cross curricular Worksheet S1.5: *It's winter, It's cold, It's cloudy, It's snowy, It's spring, It's warm, It's sunny, mummy, babies, yellow*

- **Display and talk about the worksheet:** Point and say: *Look! It's winter. Here's a bear asleep in her cave. What's the weather like? Is it cold and cloudy and snowy or warm and sunny? Look in this picture, it's spring! Here's a mummy bear playing with two baby bears. Is it cold and snowy or warm and sunny?*
- **Practise the tasks:** Call children out. Point to the picture of the bear in her cave and say: *What's the weather like here? Good. It's cold and cloudy and snowy. Draw some clouds and some snow.* Point to the picture of the bear in spring and say: *What about this picture? Is it cold and cloudy and snowy or warm and sunny? Good. It's warm and sunny. Draw the sun in the sky. What colour is the sky? Good. Colour the sky blue.*

> **Table Time**
> - The children draw clouds and snow falling in the first picture and draw and colour the sun and a blue sky in the second.
> - Encourage the children to use English to talk about the pictures.

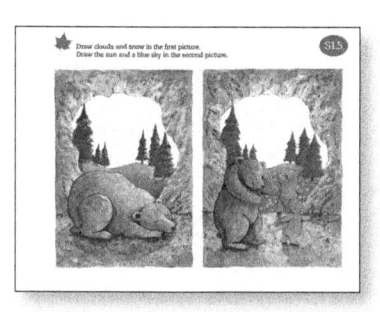

The king and the magic clothes

Name:

The king and the magic clothes

VOCABULARY AND LANGUAGE

house, shops, school, hospital
trousers, shirts, shoes, socks, hat, jacket
fire fighter, police officer, teacher, doctor
The king has lots of...
Look at my beautiful clothes.
We can make magic clothes.
Only clever people can see them.
I want magic clothes!
Not today, tomorrow.
I'm not silly. I'm clever!
Do you like my beautiful magic clothes?
Oh yes! They are very beautiful!
Look! The king has no clothes!

AUDIOS

Traditional story: *The king and the magic clothes* 5

Story song: *Look at me!* 6

Look and see! Look and see!
I'm as handsome as can be!
Come out of your houses.
Come out of your shops.
Come out of your schools.
And look at me!

Story music 7

You're making the magic clothes. Stop.
You're giving the magic clothes to the king. Stop.
Now you're the king. You're putting on the clothes. Stop.
You're in the street waving to the people. Stop.
Oops! You're going to your palace... quickly. Stop.

Traditional story: *The king and the magic clothes*: Student´s version 8

Songs to revise:

Hair, hands, feet and toes	1.32
Wake up!	2.6
Close your eyes	2.1
We´re off	2.11
One finger, one thumb, keep moving	3.9
She'll be coming round the mountain	3.12
The wheels on the bus	3.15

Also:

I can paint a picture	1.22
Where's mummy?	1.27
Do you know your numbers?	1.13
Tommy thumb	3.1
Five little ducks	3.4
Tina´s gym	1.7

The king and the magic clothes

MATERIALS

- Flashcards: *house, shops, school, hospital, trousers, shirts, shoes, socks, hat, jacket, fire fighter, police officer, teacher, doctor, teddy, dolly, ball, monster, bike, game, robot, scooter, picture*
- Big Jungle flashcards: *vain, grumpy, sleepy, happy, sad, cupboard, clever, clothes, shirt, money*
- Flashcards: *vain and clever* (Presentation of the story)
- An arrow or a crown made from stiff card. If you decide to use the crown, cut out the crown from page 1 and stick it onto card (While reading activities).
- Big Book and flashcard for *vain* (Story song)
- A pile of clothes and relevant objects for the characters, for example: a paper crown (see Art and craft activities), a toy stethoscope, a book, a whistle, black rubber boots or the flashcards: *fire fighter, police officer, teacher, doctor* (Acting out the story)
- A world map or preferably a globe and photos cut out from magazines or downloaded from the internet of men, women, boys and girls in Western clothes and traditional dresses from different cultures around the world. (Cross curricular activities)
- Photos from magazines or downloaded from the internet of people wearing clothes from different cultures. A world map. Punchers or scissors. Sellotape or Blu tack and brightly coloured wool. (Cross curricular activities: **Clothes from around the world poster**)
- Pictures of old fashioned and of modern toys from magazines or downloaded from the internet. Look for traditional games too: jacks, marbles, skipping games, hopscotch… which you can teach the children to play. (Cross curricular activities: **Toys and games, old and modern**)
- As many strips of card of about 55 cms long and 12 cms wide as you have children in the class. Draw a zig zag line along the top of the strips of card for children to cut along, to make the points of the crown. A stapler or sellotape and *gomets*, paints, glitter and so on, for decoration. (Art and craft activities: **A crown**)

The king and the magic clothes

Presentation of the story

- Show the children the Big Book. Ask them to guess who is in today's story. Use Tommy to help you draw a crown bit by bit on the board. Ask the children to guess what you are drawing. Each time repeat what children say in English. Say: *Yes, the story is about a king.* Show the flashcard for *vain* and see if the children remember the word from *The princess and the pea*. Say: *He's a very vain king!*
- **Introduce the story:** Show the children the picture of the king on the first page. Encourage the children to imitate him, patting and admiring their clothes in a mirror. Encourage them to say with you *Look at my beautiful clothes!*

While listening activities

* **First reading** (you need the flashcard *clever*)
  - You can go through the story commenting and asking children to tell you what they can see in the pictures, encouraging them to do this in English until you get to page 19. Ask the children what they think the men are saying. Tell them they are offering some magic clothes to the king. Ask them to predict how the clothes are magic. Show the flashcard *clever* and establish the meaning giving more examples / explaining in the children's mother tongue that the clothes are magic because only clever people can see them. Silly people can't! Ask *Do you think the king wants the magic clothes?* Tell the children they are going to listen to the story to find out and play the story on the audio. Alternatively, play the audio and show the pages one by one, pausing to ask questions. Point to the characters and mime to help comprehension. Repeat children's answers in English as necessary.

> **QUESTIONS:**
>
> Pages 16 and 17: — *What does the king have in his cupboard?*
> Page 19: — *How are the clothes magic?*
> (show children the flashcard for *clever* and make sure they understand the concept)
> *Does the king want the magic clothes?*
> Pages 21, 22 and 23: — *Does the king / Do the doctor and the teacher / the fire fighter and the police officer say they can see the clothes? Why?*
> Pages 26 and 27, ask: — *What does the child say?*
> *Where does the king go?*
> *Is he clever or silly?*

The king and the magic clothes

Subsequent readings

- Call a child out to help you turn the pages.
- Put the *happy* and *sad* flashcards on the board and as you tell the story ask the children if the characters are happy or sad and why. Repeat what they say in English.
- Show a page and call children out to stick the story arrow / crown on: *The King, the servant, blue trousers, a black hat, a yellow jacket, the two men, the bag of money* before or after you read the page.
- Put the flashcards: *teddy, dolly, ball, monster, bike, game, robot, scooter* on the carpet / board. Ask children questions like: *Do you remember seeing a ball in the story?* Make two piles, the ones they remember seeing and the ones they don't. Before you read each page ask children to look and see if any of the objects on the flashcards are on the page. (The only ones that aren't there are *monster, game and robot.*)
- Before the class, cover some of the characters and objects with post its. As you read the story the children say who or what is behind the post its.
- Encourage the children to join in with the actions of the story and with some of the lines, for example: *I'm not silly! I'm clever! Do you like my magic clothes? Yes, very beautiful clothes! Ha, ha, ha! The king has no clothes!* You can use Polly for this. First Polly imitates the characters and their voices and then the children join in saying it again. You can make this into a chant. Polly says a line in a rhythmic fashion, the children repeat it, for example:

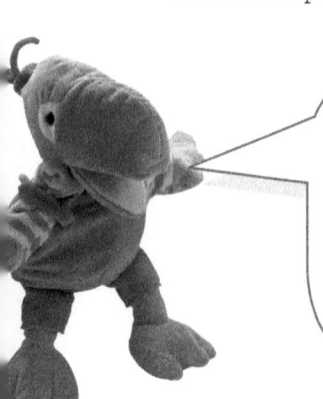

> (Polly) *Do you like*
> (children) *Do you like*
> (Polly) *my magic clothes?*
> (children) *my magic clothes?*
> continue with *Yes, very beautiful clothes! I'm not silly! I'm clever!*

- Say a sentence from the story and turn the pages. The children say *Stop* when you get to the appropriate page.
- Tell the story making mistakes for children to correct, for example, Page 1… *The king loves toys.* (No! Clothes) Page 2: *The king has lots of shoes and socks.* (No! Trousers, shirts and hats). You can use Tommy to do this activity.

After listening activities

* **Story song: *Look at me!*** 6 You need the Big Book and the flashcard for *vain*.

  - Show page 18 and the flashcard for *vain*. Ask the children what they think the king is singing. Work out mimes for each line (for example, pat your hair and clothes for *I'm as handsome as can be*). Say the song encouraging the children to join in with the mimes.
  - Sing the song: Play the song on the CD and encourage the children to join in the mimes and words.
  - Sing the song pausing for the children to sing the next word(s), for example: *I'm as… as can be, Come out of your… Look at…*
  - Sing the song but make mistakes, for example: *I'm as vain as can be. Come out of your hospitals / gardens / cupboards.* The children correct you.
  - Ask a volunteer to act as the king while the rest of the class sing his song.

* **Musical numbers**

  - Establish mimes for items of clothing, for example, shirt: shake your arms; hat: take a hat off and put it on again; trousers: wiggle your bottom; socks: pull up imaginary socks; shoes: stamp your feet; jacket: shrug your shoulders. Write 1 and 2 on opposite sides of the board. Say: *Shoe. How many shoes do we wear?* Children say and point to 2. Put on some music. The children stamp their feet to the music. Pause the music and say: *Shirt. How many shirts do we wear?* The children say and point to 1 and then shake their arms to the music. Continue with other items of clothing.

Story Pictionary

- Start drawing something that is in the story. The children guess what it is, name it and find a page in the book where it appears.

Acting out the characters

- Look through the book with the children and ask them to tell you the characters (the king, the two men, the servant, the doctor, the teacher, the fire fighter, the police officer and the children). Mime wringing your hands together and then stretching out imaginary clothes. Ask the children: *Who am I?* Continue with the other characters. Children can volunteer to take over your role. They whisper to you before acting out the character so you can help them!

The king and the magic clothes

Activities to practise the vocabulary from the story

1) Using flashcards

* **Flashcards:** hat, jacket, books, scarf, trousers, T-shirt, dress, socks, shoes, jumper, shorts, sandals, swimsuit, sunglasses, shirt
  * **Clothes game with Polly**: Tell the children that Polly wants to play at being the king. Tuck a flashcard under her arm and say in a Polly voice: *Look at my beautiful clothes. Look at my beautiful...* Show the children the picture and they finish the sentence in a Polly voice. Continue with other clothes.
  * Put the *cupboard* flashcard on the floor and ask questions: *Was there a hat in the king's cupboard?* Put under the cupboard flashcard the clothes the children say are in his cupboard. When you have gone through all the clothes check with pages 16 and 17.
  * Look at pages 16 and 17 with the children and say: *Let's help the king choose his clothes.* Children make suggestions. Check with page 18 what the king chose.
  * Flashcards *police officer, fire fighter, doctor, hospital, school, shop*.
    Hide one of the job flashcards under one of the place flashcards. Ask questions like: *Where is the police officer?* Children take it in turns to guess. If they are right, show them the flashcard. If they are wrong, say: *No he isn't.* Children can take over your role.
  * For more flashcard games see page 25.

* **Story flashcards** *clothes, shirt, money, clever, vain, grumpy, sleepy, sad, happy*
  * Show children the shirt flashcard and ask: *What is the difference between shirt and T-shirt?* (a T-shirt doesn't have a collar). Put the *clothes* and the *shirt* flashcards on the board / carpet. Show children the *money* flashcard and hide it behind the clothes or the shirt flashcard. Children guess where it is.
  * Show the flashcard *clever* and go through the characters in the story, pointing to them in the book and discussing with the children if they are clever or not. Repeat what they say in English.
  * Sing the song **Are you feeling sad today** from level 2 using the flashcards *clever, vain, grumpy, sleepy, sad, happy* as prompts for the children to sing the verses.
  * For more flashcard games see page 25.

* **Vocabulary Worksheet S2.4** See page 48.

2) Story music 7

Say: *You're making the magic clothes. / You're giving the magic clothes to the king. / Now you're the king. You're putting on the clothes. / You're in the street waving to the people. / Oops! You're going to your palace quickly.*

* Say the phrases and mime them for the children to join in.
* Practise the actions without the music: Name children to come out and mime the actions of the story with you. Then all the children mime at the same time. To make this more fun say *Stop* and the children freeze between mimes.
* Play the story music and the children follow the instructions.

The king and the magic clothes

(3) **Story Worksheets S2.1 S2.2 S2.3**.
See **Presenting the worksheets** section on page 48.

Note: The children should complete these worksheets before they do: Traditional story: *The king and the magic clothes*: Student´s version (8)

★ **Traditional story: *The king and the magic clothes*: Student´s version** (8)
- Listen to the audio: Children open their books and follow the story. Pause the CD to turn the page. Encourage the children to follow the story, to join in with the phrases they practised with Polly and to sing the song.
- Games:

1
Say for example: *Where's the hospital? One, two, three.* The children look for the page in their books where there is a hospital. Continue with words and phrases, for example: *the fire fighter / the king's clothes in a cupboard / the king's magic clothes / the king asks the police officer and the firefighter "Do you like my magic clothes?" / The king has no clothes!*

2
Flash a page of the book again and again, first very fast and then more slowly. Children say what they can see.

3
Choose a page. Children guess what is on it.

★ **Acting out the story Worksheet S2.6.** (See Materials).
The children act out the story using: *The king and the magic clothes*: Student´s version (8):
- The children press out the king and his clothes. (**Worksheet S2.6.**)
- Encourage them to put the king's clothes on and then take them off as they listen to the story. Play the CD.
- Call out children to play the part of the king, the two men, the doctor, the teacher, the police officer, the fire fighter and the child. Each of the characters brings the relevant object or flashcard.
- Establish in the classroom where the palace and the town are.
- The story can start with the king trying on the clothes and admiring himself in the mirror.
- Read the part of the narrator and encourage the children to act out the story and to repeat expressions after you. Repeat with a different group of children.

The king and the magic clothes

Cross curricular activities

1. Clothes from around the world:
You need all the clothes flashcards, a globe and photos of people wearing different clothes. (see Materials)

- Play some flashcard games to revise the clothes.
- Show the children the world map / globe and look for Spain. If there are children in the class who come from or have visited other countries look for these on the globe with the class. You can put a different coloured *gomet* on the countries so that children can find them again after the class.
- Show the children the pictures of people dressed in different ways. For each photo ask children to say what the person is wearing using the flashcards to help them. Show children on the globe where the people come from.
- Play a game. Describe the clothes of one of the people and the children look for the photo: *Find a man with a brown hat / a woman with a long dress with many colours / a girl with fur boots / a boy with a round hat.*
- If there are children from other parts of the world you can ask them to bring in traditional clothes or photos of these from their country to show the rest of the class. If their parents are willing, they can come and show the children how people in their country wear these.
- **Cross Curricular Worksheet S2.5.** See **Presenting the worksheets** section on page 48.
- **Making a clothes from around the world poster**
- The children use punchers or scissors to cut around the photos from the magazines.
- Stick a world map on the wall of the classroom. Decide with the children which country/continent the people they have cut out from the photos come from. They stick the photos around the world map and attach them to the country or continent with a piece of wool.

2. Toys and games, old and new
You need pictures of old and modern toys and games.
(See Materials)

- Show the children the pictures of the toys and games. Ask them to divide them into ones that they have or they know and ones they haven't or they don't know. Do they know how to play the different games? See if there are any toys they can match: an old fashioned toy car, a modern toy car. Ask: *What is your favourite old / modern toy?*
- Arrange to show them how to play some traditional games they don't know in the next break in the playground.

Art and craft

1. Children can choose the scene they like best in the story and draw it. Go round and ask them what is happening in their pictures. Repeat what they say in English.

2. Children can make a crown (see Materials). They cut out the triangles of the zig zag lines to make the points of the crown and decorate them with *gomets*, paints and glitter. If you want to practise shapes, draw these on the crowns for children to colour or ask them to draw them themselves. When the crowns are finished describe a crown, for example: **It has blue triangles and pink circles.** Children say which crown it is.

The king and the magic clothes

PRESENTING THE WORKSHEETS

✻ **Story worksheet S2.1 (Sides A and B)** trousers, shirts, hats, jackets, pyjamas, colours, circle.
Look at my beautiful clothes. I want magic clothes!

- **Revise:** the clothes and triangle, circle, rectangle with flashcard games.
- **Display and talk about the worksheets:** *Look, here are the king's jackets and his shoes. Here is the king. He's saying: Look at my wonderful clothes!* Show Side B of the worksheet and say: *Here is the king and here are the two men. Do you remember what they are saying? We can make magic clothes. Does the king want magic clothes? What does he say? Yes, I want magic clothes!*
- **Practise the task.** Call out children and say: *Let's decorate the king's pyjamas. Now let's finish colouring his jacket. Turn over the page. Can you find a circle? Good, follow it with your pencil.*

> **Table Time**
> - The children decorate the king's pyjamas and finish colouring his jacket. They find and trace two circles.
> - Encourage the children to say the clothes words, colours and phrases from the story.

✻ **Story worksheet S2.2 (Sides A and B):** teddy, car, scooter, ball, money, picture, *Not today. Tomorrow! Here are your magic clothes. I'm not silly! I'm clever! Very beautiful clothes!*

- **Revise** teddy, car, scooter, ball, money, picture with flashcard games.
- **Display and talk about the worksheets:** *Look, here are the two men. The king is giving them some money. He wants to see his clothes. What do the men say? Not today, tomorrow!*
  Show Side B of the worksheet and say: *The men are showing the king the magic clothes. What do they say? Are there any clothes? Good, no. But what does the king say?*
- **Practise the task:** Ask questions about the toys (open the Big Book if needed): *Where is the teddy / car? What colour is it? Turn over the page. Who has the scooter in the story, the boy or the girl? What toy does the girl have?*

> **Table Time**
> - The children trace the rectangle, triangle and circle.

✻ **Story worksheet S2.3 (Sides A and B):** hospital, school, shop, house, yellow, pink, green, orange.
Ha! Ha! Ha! The king has no clothes. Is the king clever or silly?

- **Revise** hospital, school, shop, house, yellow, pink, green, orange with flashcard games.
- **Display and talk about the worksheets** Say: *Look here is the king and the teacher, fire fighter, police officer and doctor. The little boy is saying Ha! Ha! Ha! The king has no clothes!* Show side B of the worksheet and say: *Where is the king going? Back to his palace. What are all the people doing? Yes, they are laughing.*
- **Practise the tasks:** Call a child out (use the Big Book if needed). Ask them: *Where is the (hospital)? Where are the houses? What colour is the hospital? And the shop? Get an orange crayon and colour the shop. And the school? Get a yellow crayon and colour the school. Turn the page over. Do you think the king is clever or silly? Colour your answer here.*

The king and the magic clothes

Table Time

- The children colour the shop and the school as in the story. They colour the square *clever* or *silly* according to whether they think the king is clever or not.
- Encourage the children to identify the characters and to say words and phrases from the story.
- Sing the song or play it on the CD as the children are working and encourage them to join in.

❋ **Vocabulary Worksheet S2.4:** (You need the colour flashcards) **clothes, shirt, money, king, two men, colours**

- **Display and talk about the worksheet:** Point to the pictures and ask the children questions. Ask: *Who is the king giving the money to? Yes, the men. What can you see in the cupboard? Yes, clothes, shirts, hats and shoes. What colour are the (shoes)*
- **Practise the tasks:** Call a child out. Point to the money bag and ask: *What is this? Yes, money. Who is the king giving the money to? Yes, the men. Follow the line from the king to the men with your finger.* Point to the shirts and hats and shoes in the cupboard and ask the class: *What colour is missing?* Use the colour flashcards to eliminate the colours of the clothes. *Let's colour the king's shirt purple.*

Table Time

- Use yellow *gomets* to show the king giving the money to the men. Look at the clothes on the king and in the cupboard. Colour the king's shirt the missing colour (purple).
- Point to the characters in turn and ask *Is he clever?* Encourage the children to say words in English about the pictures.

❋ **Cross curricular 2.5:** *woman, man, boy, girl, shirt, hat, jacket, dress, shoes, boots, trousers*

- **Display and talk about the worksheet:** Point and say: *Look! Here is a woman and a man, and a boy and a girl. What is the (woman) wearing? Can you see (any boots)? Where do you think the (woman) is from?*
- **Practise the tasks:** Call children out. Point to the top half of the woman and say: *Can you see the bottom half of the woman? Good. Draw a line with your finger. Colour the boy's clothes.*

Table Time

- The children match the top and the bottom halves of the people and colour the boy's clothes as they like.
- Encourage them to say the clothes words and to talk about the pictures in English.

The three Billy Goats

Name:

The three Billy Goats

VOCABULARY AND LANGUAGE

sheep, pig, cow, chicken, cat, dog
river, bridge, grass
farm, animals, brothers, monster, orange, banana
little, middle, big, special, clever, lovely, long, green, grumpy
live, eat, look, find, see, cross, go, hear, wait, begin
under, on, behind
eyes as big as oranges, a nose as long as a banana
Who's that walking / trip tripping / clip clopping
/ stamp stamping on my bridge?
I'll eat you for my breakfast.
My big brother is behind me!
He's bigger and better to eat!
Yummy! Yummy! This grass is good! Yes it is!
Let's see!

AUDIOS

Traditional story: *The three Billy Goats* 9

Story song: *The three Billy Goats.* 10
Who's that walking on my bridge?
On my bridge
On my bridge
Who's that walking on my bridge?
I'll eat you for my breakfast!

Who's that trip, tripping on my bridge?

Who's that clip, clopping on my bridge?

Who's that stamp, stamping on my bridge?

Story music: 11
You're the monster. Stop.
You're Little Billy Goat trip tripping on the bridge. Stop.
You're the monster. Stop.
You're Middle Billy Goat clip clopping on the bridge. Stop.
You're the monster. Stop.
You're Big Billy Goat stamp stamping on the bridge. Stop.
Push the monster into the river. Stop.
Eat the lovely green grass. Stop.

Traditional story: *The three Billy Goats: Student´s version* 12

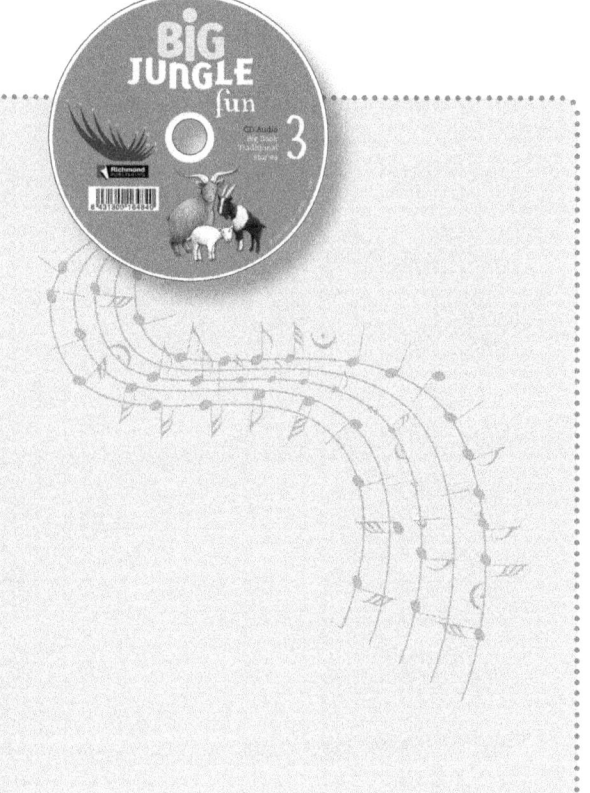

The three Billy Goats

Songs to revise

Roll over	2.21	She'll be coming round the mountain	3.12
Three Big Pizzas	2.16	The wheels on the bus	3.15
Flying high	2.26	I can paint a picture	1.22
Today is Monday	3.18	Where's mummy?	1.27
There was an old lady	3.21	Do you know your numbers?	1.13
I can sing a rainbow	3.24	Tommy thumb	3.1
Hair, hands, feet and toes	1.32	Five little ducks	3.4
Wake up!	2.6	Tina's gym	1.7
We're off	2.11		

MATERIALS

- Flashcards: *sheep, pig, cow, chicken, cat, dog, fish, monkey, lion, bear, river, tree, flower, sun, mountain, sea, beach, rainbow, star, moon, apple, banana, pear, orange, biscuit, sandwich, yoghurt, cheese, ham, tomato*
- Big Jungle flashcards: *clever, grumpy, strong, happy, sad, wood, goat, monster, bridge, grass*
- The animal flashcards (including *goat*), *clever, strong* (Presentation of the story)
- A story arrow or the monster made from stiff card. If you decide to use the monster, photocopy, cut out the monster from page 5 and stick it onto card. You can use his nose as a pointer! (While reading activities).
- Flashcards: *goat, monster, bridge, grass, wood* (Activities to practise new flashcards)
- Big Book and flashcards: *goat, bridge, monster,* a blanket / coat and two chairs (Story song)
- Flashcards: *monster, bridge* and *grass,* a blanket / coat and two chairs. (Acting out the story)
- Pictures of goats from magazines or downloaded from the internet. Look for different types of goats, mountain goats and goats from hot countries, goats of different colours, goats with different shaped horns. Goat mothers with kids (2 or maximum 3). Goats eating plants or any interesting pictures (Cross curricular activities)
- Pictures of goats as above but more of them for the areas you and the children choose to concentrate on (Cross curricular activities: **Investigating goat´s poster**)
- Books or pictures downloaded from the internet of stories with monsters, for example, *Beauty and the Beast,* witches, *Sleeping Beauty, Snow White and the seven dwarfs, Hansel and Gretel, Rapunzel;* and giants, for example: *Jack and the Beanstalk* (Cross curricular activities: **Stories with monsters, witches and giants**)
- Draw a river and a bridge on continuous paper. Make outlines or photocopies of the monster and the three Billy Goats as well as the other animals in the story (Art and craft activities: **Making a story poster**)

The three Billy Goats

Presentation of the story

(Including goat and the flashcards: *clever, strong grumpy*)

- Show the animal flashcards and ask the children to say which of the animals live on a farm. Once they have separated the farm animals, say *Today's story is about farm animals. Is it a (cow)? No, it isn't. Is it a goat? Yes, it is!*
- Sing the song: **Are you feeling happy today?** from Level 2 but including the words *clever, strong* and *grumpy*. Tell the children that in the story today there is someone clever, someone strong and someone grumpy. Put the flashcards on the board and at the end of the story ask them to tell you who is *(clever: the three Billy Goats, strong: Big Billy Goat, grumpy: the monster)*.
- **Introduce the story:** Show them the first page and say: *Look! Here are three goats. They are brothers. This is Little Billy Goat. This is Middle Billy Goat and this is Big Billy Goat.* Encourage them to say the names of the goats with you.

While listening activities

✱ First reading

You can go through the story commenting and asking children to tell you what they can see in the pictures, encouraging them to do this in English until you get to page 32. Ask the children how they think the Billy Goats are planning to get across the bridge. Repeat their predictions in English. Tell the children they are going to listen to the story to find out. Play the story on the audio. Alternatively, play the audio and show the pages one by one, pausing to ask questions. Point to the characters and mime to help comprehension. Repeat the children's answers in English as necessary.

QUESTIONS:

Page 29: — *Where is the lovely long green grass?*
Page 30: — *Why can't the animals cross the river?*
Pages 31 and 32: — *Who goes on the bridge?*
What does the monster say?
What does the Billy Goat say?
Pages 34 and 35: — *What does the monster say?*
Page 37: — *What does the monster say?*
What does Big Billy Goat say?
Page 38: — *What does Big Billy Goat do?*
Page 39: — *What do the Billy Goats eat?*
Page 40: — *What do the Billy Goats say to the other animals?*
Do they see the monster again?

The three Billy Goats

Subsequent readings

- Call a child out to help you turn the pages.
- Put the *happy* and *sad* flashcards on the board and as you tell the story ask the children if the characters are happy or sad and why. Repeat what they say in English.
- Show a page and call children out to stick the story arrow / monster on: *Middle Billy Goat, a cow, a chicken, a dog, a cat, a tree, the sun, a mountain, a bridge, a monster, eyes as big as oranges, a nose as big as a banana, the long green grass* before or after you read the page.
- Put the flashcards: *river, tree, flower, sun, mountain, sea, beach, rainbow, star, moon* on the carpet / board. Ask children questions like: *Do you remember seeing a rainbow in the story?* Make two piles, the ones they remember seeing and the ones they don't. Before you read each page ask children to look and see if any of the objects on the flashcards are on the page. (The only ones that aren't there are *sea* and *beach*).
- Encourage the children to join in with the actions of the story and with some of the lines, for example: *Little Billy Goat goes trip trip trip (to the other side of the bridge). I'm little! You can go. He is bigger and better! Yummy! Yummy! This grass is good!* You can use Polly for this. First Polly imitates the characters and their voices and then the children join in saying it again. You can make this into a chant. Polly shows the flashcard for *grass* and says in a rhythmic fashion, the children repeating:

> (Polly) *lovely*
> (children) *lovely*
> (Polly) *long*
> (children) *long*
> (Polly) *green grass*
> (children) *green grass*
> (Polly) *lovely, long, green grass*
> (children) *lovely, long, green grass*

- Say a sentence from the story and turn the pages. The children say *Stop* when you get to the appropriate page.
- Tell the story making mistakes for children to correct, for example: page 1 *Little Billy Goat, Middle Billy Goat and Big Billy Goat live in a city.* (No! A farm) *They live alone. There are no other animals.* (No! There are... See how many animals children can remember) You can use Tommy to do this activity.
- Establish mimes for the three Billy Goats and the monster (see **Acting Out the Characters** below). Tell them to listen and do the mimes every time they hear the words.
- Before the class cover some of the characters with post-its. As you read the story the children say who is behind the post-its.

After listening activities

* **Story song: *The monster's song!*** 10
  (you need flashcards: *bridge, monster*)

  - Show page 31. Do mimes for the characters (see **Acting out the characters** below) and show the flashcard for *bridge*. Establish mimes for: *bridge, I'll eat you for my breakfast, walk, trip, clop* and *stamp*.
  - Sing the song: Play the song on the CD and encourage the children to join in. Sing the song pausing before the word *bridge* for children to sing it.
  - Say for example: *Big Billy Goat* and sing the appropriate verse with the children.
  - Sing the song but make mistakes, for example: *Who's that jump jumping on my bridge? I'll eat you for my dinner.* The children correct you.
  - Make a "bridge" with a coat between two chairs. Children can take it in turn to sit underneath the coat with the monster flashcard, singing the song along with rest of the class.
  - Play a mime game with ways of going over a bridge (*tip-toe, walk, run, jump*...). Name a child to choose an action and sing the song: *Who's that (tip-toeing) on my bridge* with the class.

* **Story Pictionary**
  Start drawing something that is in the story. Children guess what it is, name it and find a page in the book where it appears.

* **Acting out the characters**
  Look through the book with the children and ask them to tell you the characters (the three Billy Goats and the monster). Establish some mimes for *Little Billy Goat, Middle Billy Goat* and *Big Billy Goat* (for example, children draw little, medium sized and big curly horns in the air beside their heads) and the monster (for example, crouch down and move from one foot to the other). Say a character's name and put on some music. The children do the mime. Say *Stop* and repeat with other characters.

The three Billy Goats

Activities to practise the vocabulary from the story

1) Using flashcards

Flashcards: Categories Race: Use all the animal, nature and countryside and food flashcards. Put them down in three piles on the carpet. Call out three children. Give them Tommy, Tina or Polly. Say for example: *Tommy, find the bear; Tina, find the rainbow; Polly, find the orange. 1. 2. 3. Go!* The children take their characters to find the flashcards and bring them to you. Repeat with other children and flashcards.
- For more flashcard games see page 25.

Story flashcards *goat, monster, bridge, grass* (take in the *wood* flashcard too)
- Put the *grass* and the *bridge* flashcards on the board / carpet. Show children the *monster* flashcards and hide one behind each of the other flashcards. Ask: *Where's the monster?* Encourage the children to guess *bridge* or *grass*. Repeat with *goat*.
- Put the flashcard for *bridge* in the middle of the board with the flashcard for *grass* on one side and the flashcard for *wood* on the other. Draw more grass after the wood. Put the monster flashcard face down. Tell a little story using the *goat* flashcard and mime: *Here's a little goat. It goes swish swish through the grass and trip trip trip trip over the bridge and whooo whooo through the wood and swish swish through the grass. Turn the monster card over. Oh no! There's a monster! Run, little goat! He goes swish swish through the grass, whooo whooo through the wood, trip trip trip trip over the bridge, swish swish through the grass and phew... he's safe!*
- The children join in with the mimes and the words.
- For more flashcard games see page 25.

Vocabulary Worksheet S3.1
See **Presenting the worksheets** section on page 58.

2) Story music 10

Say: *Everyone, you're the monster. / You're Little Billy Goat trip tripping on the bridge. / You're the monster. / You're Middle Billy Goat clip clopping on the bridge. / You're the monster. / You're Big Billy Goat stamp stamping on the bridge. / Push the monster into the river. / Eat the lovely green grass.*

- Say the phrases and mime them for the children to join in.
- Practise the actions without the music: Name children to come out and mime the actions of the story with you. Then all the children mime at the same time. To make this more fun say *Stop* and the children freeze between mimes.
- Play the story music and the children follow the instructions.

The three Billy Goats

(3) **Story Worksheets S1.1 S1.2 S1.3**. See **Presenting the worksheets** section on page 58.
Note: The children should complete these worksheets before they do: Traditional story: *The three Billy Goats*: Student´s version (3.29)

❊ **Traditional story:** *The three Billy Goats*: **Student´s version** (11)
- Listen to the audio: Children open their books and follow the story. Pause the CD to turn the page. Encourage the children to follow the story, to join in with the phrases they practised with Polly and to sing the song.
- Games:

1

Say for example, *Where's the monster? One, two, three.* The children look for the page in their books with the monster. Continue with words and phrases: *Where's the lovely long grass / Middle Billy Goat / the farm animals eating the lovely long grass. / I'll eat you for my breakfast! / Yummy! Yummy! This grass is good! / Big Billy Goat pushes the monster into the river.*

2

Flash a page of the book again and again, first very fast and then more slowly. Children say what they can see.

3

Choose a page. Children guess what is on it.

❊ **Acting out the story Worksheet S3.6** You need the *monster*, *bridge* and *grass* flashcards, a blanket / coat and two chairs.
- The children act out the story using: *The three Billy Goats*: Student´s version (11):
- The children press out the three Billy Goats puppets. (**Worksheet S3.6.**).
- Encourage them to move them as they listen to the story. Play the CD.
- Put the *grass* flashcard on one wall of the classroom and call out 3 children to be the 3 Billy Goats and stand by the opposite wall. Each of the Billy Goats can hold the relevant puppet. In the middle, between the walls, build a bridge with the blanket and two chairs. Put the flashcard of the *bridge* on it. Call out a child to play the part of the monster and sit under the bridge with the *monster* flashcard.
As you retell the story the relevant Billy Goat can cross the "bridge" with two fingers. They should do it imitating *trip tripping / clip clopping / stamp stamping*. The challenge is not to let the blanket fall!
- Read the part of the narrator and encourage the children to act out the story and to repeat expressions after you. Repeat with a different group of children.

The three Billy Goats

Cross curricular activities

1 **Investigating the real life of goats:** (See Materials)

- Ask children what they know about goats. Repeat what they say in English. Tell them that goats are very clever, they can learn to walk on a lead like a dog and open gates by themselves. They can also climb trees!
- Ask some questions: *What colour are goats? What do goats look like? Where do goats live? What do goats eat? How many babies do mummy goats have? What can we get from goats?*
- For each question show the children relevant photos:
  - *Goats can be white, brown, red, black or a mixture of these colours.*
  - *Goats look a bit like sheep. They have two horns that can be many shapes.*
  - *Goats can live almost everywhere from cold mountains to hot countries.*
  - *Goats eat almost every plant! (They even try clothes and buttons!, so watch out!)*
  - *Goats typically have twins but they can also have one baby or three babies.*
  - *You can drink goat's milk or make goat's butter or cheese. (You can also eat them and make things with their skins).*
- **Cross Curricular Worksheet S1.5.** See **Presenting the worksheets** section on page 48.
- **Making an information about goats poster** (see Materials)
- Decide with the children what information to have on your goat poster (where they live, what they eat, what they look like, what they give us, goat families, interesting information about goats).
- Divide the poster into sections depending on how many areas you are going to work on. The children use punchers or scissors to cut around the photos from the magazines and draw pictures to decorate the poster.

2 **Stories with witches, monsters and giants** (You need books or pictures representing fairy stories. See materials)

- Show the children books or pictures downloaded from the internet of fairy stories which include a witch, monster or giant. The children can categorize them into stories with witches, monsters and giants and say which ones they have read or seen. Ask *Are the witches, monsters and giants always bad?* (some might know the Wizard of Oz or more recent stories for children where there are good and bad witches) Ask: *What is your favourite story?* and ask them to tell you about it. Repeat what they say in English.
- Ask children to bring in to class story books they have at home with a witch, monster or giant in and tell an abbreviated version of the story to the children in English showing them the pictures.

Art and craft

1 Children can choose the scene they like best in the story and draw it. Go round and ask them what is happening in their pictures. Repeat what they say in English.

2 Children can make a **Poster Story.** (See Materials) Draw a river and a bridge on continuous paper. Some children can colour this brown while others draw and colour yellow grass on one side and green grass on the other. The children can draw and colour a monster, the three Billy Goats and the other farm animals (or photocopy these for them to cut out). The children can re-tell the story, moving the three Billy Goats and the monster for other classes or their parents.

The three Billy Goats

PRESENTING THE WORKSHEETS

✱ **Story Worksheet S3.1 (Sides A and B)** *goat, cow, pig, sheep, river, tree, sun, moon, stars, mountain, flower, monster, eyes, nose. Look at the lovely long green grass! Who's that trip, tripping on my bridge? I'll eat you for my breakfast. My brother is behind me. He's bigger and better!*

- **Revise the animals and countryside flashcards** with flashcard games.
- **Display and talk about the worksheets:** Point and say: *Look! Here is the moon and a star and here are the three Billy Goats looking at the grass on the other side of the river. What do they say? Yes. Look at the lovely long green grass! Why can't they go over the bridge? Yes, here is the grumpy monster under the bridge.* Show Side B of the worksheet and say: *Here is Little Billy Goat going over the bridge. What does the monster say? Yes, Who's that trip, tripping on my bridge? I'll eat you for my breakfast. And what does Little Billy Goat say? My brother is behind me. He's bigger and better!*
Say words in English and call children out to point to them in the pictures.
- **Practise the task.** Call out children and say: *What colour are the (cows) in the story? Look and see. Pick up a (brown) crayon and colour the cows. Trace the bridge. Turn over the page. Can you point to the goats? Finish colouring the goats. Where is the lovely green grass. Oops, that needs a bit of green too! Pick up a crayon and colour the grass. Thank you.*

> **Table Time**
> - The children trace the bridge and colour the cows. On the back of the page they finish colouring the goats and the grass.
> - Encourage them to point to, identify and say: *goat, cow, pig, sheep, river, tree, sun, moon, stars, mountain, flower, monster, eyes, nose.*
> - Play / sing the story song as children work.

✱ **Story worksheet S3.2 (Sides A and B):** *Middle / Big Billy goat, grass, monster, nose, rectangle, Who's that clip, clopping / stamp, stamping on my bridge? I'll eat you for my breakfast! Let's see!*

- **Revise** *goat, grass, monster, nose, rectangle* with flashcard games.
- **Display and talk about the worksheets:** Point and say: *Who's this? Yes, it's the monster. Oops! We need to colour his nose! The monster is saying: Who's that clip clopping on my bridge? I'll eat you for my breakfast!* Show Side B of the worksheet and say: *Who's this? It's the monster and here is Big Billy Goat. Oops, we need to finish his horns! What is the monster saying? Yes, Who's that stamp, stamping on my bridge? I'll eat you for my breakfast. What does the Big Billy Goat do here?*
- Point to things in the pictures and ask how to say them in English.
- **Practise the task.** Call out children and say: *Colour the monster's nose. Point to the grass. Pick up a green crayon. Follow the lines in the grass with your crayon. Turn the page over. Can you see a rectangle hidden in the picture? Yes, here is one. Trace it with your pencil. Let's look for another one.*

> **Table Time**
> - The children colour the nose of the monster and trace the lines on the grass.
> - On the back of the page they trace Big Billy Goat's horns and find and trace two rectangles on the bridge.
> - Encourage the children to identify and say: *Middle / Big Billy Goat, grass, monster, nose, rectangle, Who's that clip, clopping / stamp, stamping on my bridge?*

✱ **Story worksheet S3.3 (Sides A and B):** *Big Billy Goat, Middle Billy Goat, Little Billy Goat, sheep, pig, cow, chicken, cat, dog, fish, tree, rainbow. Yummy! Yummy! This grass is good! Thank you, Billy Goats.*
Have the Big Book to hand.

The three Billy Goats

- **Revise**: *the animals, tree, rainbow* with flashcard games.
- **Display and talk about the worksheets:** Point and say: *Look! Here are Big Billy Goat, Middle Billy Goat and Little Billy Goat all eating the lovely green grass. They are saying Yummy! Yummy! This grass is good! Look at the monster! He's in the river. Goodbye monster!* Show side B of the worksheet and say: *Here are the animals crossing the bridge. Are they happy now? They're saying, Thank you, Billy Goats!*
  Point to animals and countryside things in the picture and ask children to say them in English.
- **Practise the tasks:** Call children out. Show them the Big Book page 11 and say: *Can you see anything that is different? Yes, the tree! Pick up a green crayon and finish drawing the tree. Now you can colour it. Turn the page over. Look at the rainbow. What colours are missing here? Yes, red, yellow and blue. Can you finish colouring the rainbow with your crayons? Thank you.*

> **Table Time**
> - The children finish drawing the tree. They trace the rectangle and finish colouring the rainbow.
> - Encourage the children to identify the characters, animals and countryside words.
> - Sing the story song or play it on the CD as the children are working and encourage them to join in.

Vocabulary Worksheet S3.4: *goat, monster, bridge, grass, moon, sun, flower, eyes, nose*

- Play a game with the flashcards: *goat, monster, bridge, grass, moon, sun, flower, eyes, nose*
  Point to the pictures and ask the children questions. Ask: *What is this? Yes, it's a bridge. What's this? Yes, it's a star. How many stars are there here? Yes, (six). What's this? Yes, its a goat. It's Little Billy goat. And this? Yes, it's Big Billy Goat. What's this? Yes, it's grass. And this? Yes, it's a flower. How many flowers? Yes, (one). What's this? Yes, it's the monster from the story. And this monster, how many (eyes) does he have? Yes, (three).*
- **Practise the tasks:** Call a child out. Point to the first picture on the first row and ask: *What can you see? Good. A bridge and a sun. Can you find another picture the same? Yes, good. Circle the picture.* Continue in the same way with the other rows.

> **Table Time**
> - The children circle the picture in each row that is the same as the first picture.
> - Encourage the children to say: *goat, monster, bridge, grass, moon, sun, flower, eyes, nose*

Cross curricular 3.5: *white, red, brown, black, grass, plants, mountain, milk, butter, cheese*

- **Display and talk about the worksheet:** Point and say: *Look! Here is a goat. It's white. Shall we leave it white or shall we colour it? Look, here is a mother with two babies and a mother with ten babies. Here is a picture of a hot country. Here is some food, some meat and some plants. Here are things we get from goats. Here is some cheese.*
- **Practise the tasks:** Call children out. Point to the picture of the goat and say: *Colour the goat.* Point to the pictures around the goat and say: *How many babies does a goat have? Yes, two. Colour the circle around the mummy and two babies. Where can goats live? Yes, mountains. Draw some mountains here. What do goats eat? Yes, grass and plants. Colour the circle around the plants. What do goats give us? Yes, milk. Draw a glass of milk here.*

> **Table Time**
> - The children colour the goat and the circles around the mother and two babies and the grass and plants. They draw a mountain bnd a glass of milk in the empty squares.
> - Encourage the children to use English to talk about the pictures.

Audio transcripts

1.1 Hello!
Hello, hello everyone. (x2)
Hello, _____. (x4)
Hello, hello everyone. (x2)

1.2 Hello everyone
Tommy tiger says "hello".
Tina tortoise says "hello".
Polly parrot says "hello".
Hello everyone!

Hello Tommy tiger.
Hello Tina tortoise.
Hello Polly parrot.
Hello everyone!

1.3 Tidy up!
Tidy up, tidy up,
Everyone tidy up.
Put your things away,
Tidy up today.

1.4 Goodbye
Goodbye Tommy, (x3)
See you another day!

Goodbye teacher, (x3)
See you another day!

Goodbye children, (x3)
See you another day!

1.5 All together
All together come to me, (x3)
Sit down.
One, two, three!

All together look at me, (x3)
Fold your arms.
One, two, three!

1.6 Table time
Hey-ho, hey-ho, off to work we go.
We do our best,
And then we rest.
Hey-ho, hey-ho, hey-ho, hey-ho!

1.7 Tina's gym
Stand up straight,
Stretch up tall.
Wiggle your fingers,
Let your arms fall.
Bend your legs,
Touch your toes.
Wiggle your bottom,
Touch your nose.
Breathe in,
Breathe out.
Relax your body,
Shake it all about!

1.8 The weather song
What's the weather?
What's the weather?
What's the weather like today?
Is it sunny?
Is it cloudy?
Is it hot or cold today?

What's the weather?
What's the weather?
What's the weather like today?
Is it rainy?
Is it windy?
Is it hot or cold today?

1.9 The days of the week
Monday, Tuesday, Wednesday, Thursday,
Friday, Saturday, Sunday too.
One, two, three, four, five, six, seven days,
Seven days for me and you!

Audio transcripts

1.10 Colour song: All colours

Yellow, yellow, a yellow duck. (x3)
Quack! Quack! Quack!

Red, red, a red bird. (x3)
Tweet! Tweet! Tweet!

Blue, blue, a blue whale. (x3)
Psh! Psh! Psh!

Green, green, a green frog. (x3)
Ribbit! Ribbit! Ribbit!

Orange, orange, an orange fish. (x3)
Glug! Glug! Glug!

Pink, pink, a pink pig. (x3)
Oink! Oink! Oink!

Black, black, a black hen. (x3)
Cluck! Cluck! Cluck!

White, white, a white mouse. (x3)
Eek! Eek! Eek!

Brown, brown, a brown bear. (x3)
Grr! Grr! Grr!

Purple, purple, a purple snake. (x3)
Hiss! hiss! hiss!

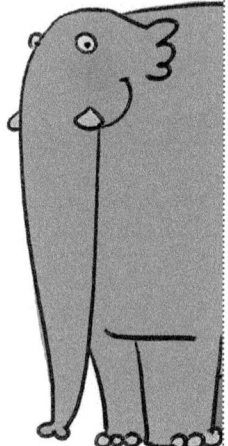

1.11 Big and little

Elephant is big, very big.
He has big ears,
And a very big nose.

Mosquito is little, very little.
She has little eyes,
And a very little mouth.

1.12 Number song: 1–10

One, one, one. Bang your drum!
Two, two, two. Touch your shoe!
Three, three, three. Touch your knee!
One, two, three. One, two, three!

Four, four, four. Touch the floor!
Five, five, five. Do a jive!
Six, six, six. Do the splits!
Four, five, six. Four, five, six!

Seven, seven, seven. Colour with a crayon!
Eight, eight, eight. Don't be late!
Nine, nine, nine. I am fine!
Ten, ten, ten. Let's sing again!

1.13 Do you know your numbers, colours and shapes? 1

Do you know your numbers, numbers, numbers?
Do you know your numbers? Let me see.
Show me 1.
Show me 2.
Show me 3.
Do you know your colours, colours, colours?
Do you know your colours? Let me see.
Show me blue.
Show me red.
Show me yellow.
Show me green.
Do you know your shapes, shapes, shapes?
Do you know your shapes? Let me see.
Show me a circle.
Show me a square.

1.14 Do you know your numbers, colours and shapes? 2

Do you know your numbers, numbers, numbers?
Do you know your numbers? Let me see.
Show me 3.
Show me 4.
Show me 5.
Do you know your colours, colours, colours?
Do you know your colours? Let me see.
Show me black.
Show me brown.
Show me white.
Show me green.
Do you know your shapes, shapes, shapes?
Do you know your shapes? Let me see.
Show me a circle.
Show me a square.
Show me a triangle.

1.15 Long and short

I've got very long legs.
And a very long neck.
I'm a giraffe and I stretch like this.
I stretch like this, (x2)
I'm a giraffe and I stretch like this.

I've got very short legs.
And a very short neck.
I'm a penguin and I walk like this.
I walk like this, (x2)
I'm a penguin and I walk like this.

Audio transcripts

1.16 *Do you know your numbers, colours and shapes? 3*

Do you know your numbers, numbers, numbers?
Do you know your numbers? Let me see.
Show me 3.
Show me 4.
Show me 5.
Show me 6.
Do you know your colours, colours, colours?
Do you know your colours? Let me see.
Show me pink.
Show me orange.
Show me purple.
Show me white.
Do you know your shapes, shapes, shapes?
Do you know your shapes? Let me see.
Show me a circle.
Show me a square.
Show me a triangle.
Show me a rectangle.

1.17 *There's a spider 1*

There's a spider on the sofa! Peek! Peek!
There's a spider on the sofa! Peek! Peek!
There's a creepy crawly spider, a creepy crawly spider!
There's a spider on the sofa! Eek! Eek!

There's a spider under the table! Peek! Peek!
There's a spider under the table! Peek! Peek!
There's a creepy crawly spider, a creepy crawly spider!
There's a spider under the table! Eek! Eek!

1.18 *Loud and quiet*

I can sing quietly.
I can walk quietly.
I can clap quietly.
I can stamp quietly.

I can sing loudly.
I can walk loudly.
I can clap loudly.
I can stamp loudly.

I can sing quietly.
I can walk quietly.
I can clap quietly.
I can stamp quietly.

1.19 *There's a spider 2*

There's a spider in the toilet! Peek! Peek!
There's a spider in the toilet! Peek! Peek!
There's a creepy crawly spider, a creepy crawly spider!
There's a spider in the toilet! Eek! Eek!

There's a spider next to the bath! Peek! Peek!
There's a spider next to the bath! Peek! Peek!
There's a creepy crawly spider, a creepy crawly spider!
There's a spider next to the bath! Eek! Eek!

1.20 *There's a spider 3*

There's a spider in front of the chair! Peek! Peek!
There's a spider in front of the chair! Peek! Peek!
There's a creepy crawly spider, a creepy crawly spider!
There's a spider in front of the chair! Eek! Eek!

There's a spider behind the bed! Peek! Peek!
There's a spider behind the bed! Peek! Peek!
There's a creepy crawly spider, a creepy crawly spider!
There's a spider behind the bed! Eek! Eek!

1.21 *Do you know your numbers, colours and shapes? 4*

Do you know your numbers, numbers, numbers?
Do you know your numbers? Let me see.
Show me 8.
Show me 4.
Show me 10.
Show me 6.
Do you know your colours, colours, colours?
Do you know your colours? Let me see.
Show me black.
Show me purple.
Show me green.
Show me brown.
Do you know your shapes, shapes, shapes?
Do you know your shapes? Let me see.
Show me a triangle.
Show me a circle.
Show me a rectangle.
Show me a square.

1.36 *The little bells of Christmas*

The little bells of Christmas say dong, dong, dong, dong-dong!
The little bells of Christmas say dong, dong, dong!
The little drums of Christmas say boom, boom, boom, boom-boom!
The little drums of Christmas say boom, boom, boom!
The triangles of Christmas say ting, ting, ting, ting-ting!
The triangles of Christmas say ting, ting, ting!
The tambourines of Christmas say brring, brring, brring, brring-brring!
The tambourines of Christmas say brring, brring, brring!

Unit 1 Audio transcripts

1.22 Action song 1: *I can paint a picture*

I can paint a picture, picture, picture.
I can paint a picture,
Look at me!

I can clean my table, table, table.
I can clean my table,
Look at me!

I can push my chair in, chair in, chair in.
I can push my chair in,
Look at me!

1.23 Tommy's music 1

Paint a picture of a table.
Tap the floor with your hand.
Read a book.
Tap the floor with your foot.
Paint a picture of a chair.
Dance with your teacher.

1.24 Story 1: *Tina's chair*

1.

Narrator: Look! Tina, Polly and Tommy are in the classroom. Here's a table and some crayons. Here's the teacher and here's a picture.
Teacher: Sit down Tina.
Tina: I can't. It's my shell! Oh! Help!

2.

Narrator: Crash bang! Oops! Oh dear! Tina is on the floor!
Tina: Oh! Ouch!
Tommy: Don't cry Tina!
Polly: Here's your chair Tina.

3.

Narrator: The teacher is talking to Tommy and Polly and Tina about the picture.
Teacher: What colour is the rubber?
Tommy: It's yellow.
Teacher: What colour is the pencil?
Polly: It's red.
Narrator: Oh dear! Look at Tina! Be careful Tina!
Tina: Oh! Help!

4.

Narrator: Crash bang! Oops! Oh dear! Tina is on the floor!
Tina: Oh! Ouch! It's my shell!
Tommy: Don't cry Tina!
Polly: Here's your chair Tina. I've got an idea!

5.

Narrator: Look at the window! Who is it?
Polly: This is my friend Woody.
Tommy: Hello Woody.
Teacher: Look at Woody. Don't cry Tina.

6.

Narrator: Look at Woody Woodpecker! He is cutting Tina's chair!
Tina: What is he doing?
Polly: Wait and see!

7.

Narrator: Look! Here's a circle in Tina's chair!
Woody: Here's your chair Tina.
Tina: Thank you, Woody!!

8.

Narrator: Ha ha! Look at Tina. Now she can sit on her chair! She's very happy!
Teacher: Colour the rubbers yellow, the pencils red and the books blue please.
Tina: Goodbye Woody!
Woody: Goodbye Tina.

1.25 Story chant 1: *Tina's chair*

Tina's on the floor
Boo! Hoo! Boo! Hoo!
Don't cry Tina!

Here comes Woody.
Hello Woody.

Here's your chair, Tina!
Thank you, Woody.
Goodbye Woody.

1.26 CONTINUOUS ASSESSMENT

Activity 1

Get the Tommy sticker and stick it next to the chair.
Get the Polly sticker and stick it next to the rubber.
Get the Tina sticker and stick it next to the picture.
Get the Petal sticker and stick it next to the book.
Get the Twig sticker and stick it next to the table.
Get the babies sticker and stick it next to the pencil.

Activity 2

Pick up a red crayon and trace the 1.
Pick up a yellow crayon and trace the circle.
Pick up a blue crayon and trace the 3.
Pick up a green crayon and trace the 2.
Pick up a red crayon and trace the square.

Unit 1   Audio transcripts

3.1   Authentic song 1: Tommy Thumb

Tommy Thumb, Tommy Thumb,
Where are you?

Here I am, here I am,
How are you?

Peter Pointer, Peter Pointer,
Where are you?

Here I am, here I am,
How are you?

Middle Man, Middle Man,
Where are you?

Here I am, here I am,
How are you?

Ruby Ring, Ruby Ring,
Where are you?

Here I am, here I am,
How are you?

Baby Small, Baby Small,
Where are you?

Here I am, here I am,
How are you?

Fingers all, fingers all,
Where are you?

Here we are, here we are,
How are you do?

3.2   Photo Poster 1: Pictures in order. Look at the poster. Listen and mime. Listen and repeat.

Hello. My name's John. I'm 5. I live in Uganda, in Africa.

This is our school. It's green and orange.
Good morning, children!
Good morning, teacher!
This is a classroom.
This is the playground.
It's a snake.
We do reading.
We do writing.
We do sums.
Every day we have a snack.

3.3   Photo Poster 1: Pictures not in order. Look at the poster. Listen and mime. Listen and repeat.

Hello. My name's John. I'm 5. I live in Uganda, in Africa.

We do sums.
This is the playground.
This is our school. It's green and orange.
We do writing.
Every day we have a snack.
It's a snake.
We do reading.
Good morning, children!
Good morning, teacher!
This is a classroom.

3.27   Activity Book Unit 1

Listen and say what's next.
1. paper   writing   book
2. pencil   reading   table
3. crayon   playground   teacher
4. floor   picture   classroom

Listen and circle what's next with a pencil.
1. paper   writing   book
2. pencil   reading   table
3. crayon   playground   teacher
4. floor   picture   classroom

Unit 2 Audio transcripts

1.27 Action song 2: *Where's Mummy?*

Where's Mummy?
There she is!
Sleeping on the sofa
Snore, snore, snore!

Where's Daddy?
There he is!
Washing in the bath.
Splash, splash, splash!

Where's my brother?
There he is!
Jumping on the bed.
Boing, boing, boing!

Naughty boy!

1.28 Tommy's music 2

You're reading a book on the sofa.
You're having a bath.
You're dancing with baby.
You're in bed. Go to sleep.

1.29 Story 2: *Petal's family*

1.

Narrator: Look! Here's Tommy and here's Petal. And here's Petal's house.
Petal: Here's my house.
Tommy: What a beautiful house!

2.

Narrator: Look at Petal's daddy! He's making the bed.
Daddy: Twinkle, winkle, twinkle, winkle, twinkle, winkle, twinkle wink.
Petal: Hello Daddy. This is Tommy.
Daddy: Hello Tommy.
Tommy: What a beautiful daddy!

3.

Narrator: Look at Petal's mummy. She's sleeping on the sofa!
Petal: Wake up Mummy! Tickle, tickle.

4.

Narrator: Now Petal's mummy is awake. She's giving the baby a bath.
Petal: Hello Mummy. This is Tommy.
Mummy: Hello Tommy.
Tommy: What a beautiful mummy! What a beautiful baby!

5.

Narrator: Look! Here's all the family. Here's Daddy and Petal, and the baby, and Mummy and here are Petal's brother and sister!
Tommy: What a beautiful brother and a beautiful sister!
Petal: Do you want a sandwich Tommy?

6.

Narrator: Uh oh! Tommy is eating all the sandwiches!
Tommy: Yummy, yummy sandwiches!

7.

Narrator: Oh dear!
Brother, sister & baby: Oh no! Boo hoo. No sandwiches!
Daddy: Oops!
Petal: Oops!
Tommy: Oops! Sorry!
Mummy: Don't worry Tommy. Twinkle winkle, twinkle winkle. Twinkle, winkle, twinkle, wink! Make a spell and do it well! One, two, three!

8.

Narrator: Oh good!
Mummy: Here are some more sandwiches.
Narrator: Now everyone is happy again!

1.30 Story chant 2: *Petal's family*

Here's Petal's daddy,
Twinkle winkle.
Here's Petal's mummy,
Twinkle winkle.
Here's Petal's brother,
Twinkle winkle.
Here's Petal's sister,
Twinkle winkle.
And here's the little baby,
Twinkle winkle, twinkle wink!

1.31 CONTINUOUS ASSESSMENT

Activity 1

Get the Petal sticker and stick it next to the sofa.
Get the Tina sticker and stick it next to the granny.
Get the Tommy sticker and stick it next to the bath.
Get the babies sticker and stick it next to the book.
Get the Twig sticker and stick it next to the brother.
Get the Polly sticker and stick it next to the daddy.

Activity 2

Pick up a black crayon and trace the triangle.
Pick up a brown crayon and trace the 3.
Pick up a blue crayon and trace the circle.
Pick up a green crayon and trace the 5.
Pick up a red crayon and trace the 4.

Unit 2 Audio transcripts

3.4 Authentic song 2: Five little ducks

Five little ducks went out one day.
Over the hill and far away.
Mummy duck said, quack, quack, quack, quack!
But only four little ducks came back.

Four little ducks went out one day.
Over the hill and far away.
Mummy duck said, quack, quack, quack, quack!
But only three little ducks came back.

Three little ducks went out one day.
Over the hill and far away.
Mummy duck said, quack, quack, quack, quack!
But only two little ducks came back.

Two little ducks went out one day.
Over the hill and far away.
Mummy duck said, quack, quack, quack, quack!
But only one little duck came back.

One little duck went out one day.
Over the hill and far away.
Mummy duck said quack, quack, quack, quack!
But no little ducks came back.

Mummy duck went out one day.
Over the hill and far away.
Mummy duck said quack, quack, quack, quack!
And five little ducks came back.

3.5 Photo Poster 2: Pictures in order. Look at the poster. Listen and mime. Listen and repeat.

Hello. My name's Emma. I'm 4. This is my family. We all help.

Emma's daddy is laying the table.
Walkies!
Emma's brother is walking the dog.
Emma's mummy is looking after the baby.
Emma's granny is making the bed.
Emma's sister is feeding the cat.
Emma's grandad is watering the plants.

3.6 Photo Poster 2: Pictures not in order. Look at the poster. Listen and mime. Listen and repeat.

Hello. My name's Emma. I'm 4. This is my family. We all help.

Emma's grandad is watering the plants.
Emma's mummy is looking after the baby.
Emma's sister is feeding the cat.
Walkies!
Emma's brother is walking the dog.
Emma's daddy is laying the table.
Emma's granny is making the bed.

3.28 Activity Book Unit 2.

Listen and say what's next.
1. walk the dog   brother   daddy
2. lay the table   grandad   sofa
3. bath   granny   make the bed
4. baby   table   sister

Listen and circle what's next with a pencil.
1. walk the dog   brother   daddy
2. lay the table   grandad   sofa
3. bath   granny   make the bed
4. baby   table   sister

Unit 3   Audio transcripts

1.32 Action song 3: *Hair, hands, feet and toes*

Hair, hands, feet and toes,
Feet and toes.
Hair, hands, feet and toes,
Feet and toes.
And eyes and ears and mouth and nose,
Hair, hands, feet and toes.
Feet and toes.

1.33 Tommy's music 3

Wash your hands.
Wash your hair.
Wash your feet.
Wash your arms.
Wash your legs.
Dance.

1.34 Story 3: *The snowman*

1.

Narrator: Look at the beautiful snowman!
Tina: I like our snowman.
Polly: I like our snowman too.
Narrator: But Tommy isn't happy.
Tommy: I don't like our snowman!
Let's make legs and feet!
Tina: Legs and feet?

2.

Narrator: Now the snowman has two legs and two feet.
Polly: I like our snowman with legs and feet!
Tina: I like our snowman with legs and feet too!
Narrator: But Tommy isn't happy.
Tommy: I don't like our snowman! Let's make arms and hands.
Polly: Arms and hands?

3.

Narrator: Now the snowman has two legs and two feet and two arms and two hands.
Tina: I like our snowman with arms and hands.
Polly: I like our snowman with arms and hands too.
Narrator: But Tommy isn't happy.
Tommy: I don't like our snowman! ... Let's make hair!
Tina & Polly: Hair?

4.

Narrator: Now the snowman has two legs and two feet and two arms and two hands and some yellow hair.
Polly: I like our snowman with yellow hair.
Tina: I like our snowman with yellow hair too!
Narrator: And Tommy is happy.
Tommy: Yes! I like our snowman too! It's a beautiful snowman!

5.

Narrator: But, oh dear! Here comes the sun!
The snowman begins to melt down, down, down.
Tommy: Oh!
Tina: Ooh!
Polly: Ooh!

6.

Narrator: And down ... and down! Tommy is sad and Tina is sad and Polly is sad.
But what are Twig and Petal doing?
Twig & Petal: Twinkle winkle,
tinkle winkle. Twinkle winkle, twinkle wink!
Make a spell and do it well. One, two, three!

7.

Tina: Look! Look at the tree!
Polly: Oh what a beautiful tree!
Tommy: And look! Presents. One, two, three presents!
There's a present for Tommy and a present for Tina and a present for Polly!

8.

Narrator: There's a snowman hat for Tina and a snowman hat for Polly and a snowman hat for Tommy.
Tommy: My hat is a snowman with two legs and two feet.
Tina: And two arms and two hands.
Polly: And yellow hair.
All: Ha, ha, ha!
Narrator: Happy Christmas everyone!

1.35 Story chant 3: *The snowman*

I like our snowman. With legs and feet.
I like our snowman. With arms and hands.
I like our snowman. With yellow hair.
It's a beautiful snowman!

1.36 *The little bells of Christmas*
(See page 62.)

1.37 CONTINUOUS ASSESSMENT

Activity 1

Get the babies sticker and stick it next to the hair.
Get the Polly sticker and stick it next to the eyes.
Get the Twig sticker and stick it next to the hands.
Get the Tina sticker and stick it next to the legs.
Get the Tommy sticker and stick it next to the mouth.
Get the Petal sticker and stick it next to the head.

Activity 2

Pick up a brown crayon and trace the long hair.
Pick up a black crayon and trace the short hair.

Unit 3   Audio transcripts

3.7 Photo Poster 3: Pictures in order. Look at the poster. Listen and mime. Listen and repeat.

Hello. My name's Charlie. I'm 5.
It's Christmas. Come to my house!

We have a Christmas tree.
We have stockings.
We have Christmas cards.
We eat turkey.
We eat Christmas pudding.
We pull crackers.
We wear paper hats.

3.8 Photo Poster 3: Pictures not in order. Look at the poster. Listen and mime. Listen and repeat.

Hello. My name's Charlie.
I'm 5. It's Christmas. Come to my house!

We have stockings.
We eat turkey.
We have a Christmas tree.
We pull crackers.
We wear paper hats.
We have Christmas cards.
We eat Christmas pudding.

3.29 Activity Book Unit 3.

Listen and say what's next.
1. leg   head   paper hat
2. hair   arm   eyes
3. nose   hands   Christmas pudding   ears
4. feet   mouth   turkey

Listen and circle what's next with a pencil.
1. leg   head   paper hat
2. hair   arm   eyes
3. nose   hands   Christmas pudding   ears
4. feet   mouth   turkey

Unit 4 Audio transcripts

2.1 Action song 4: *Close your eyes*

Close your eyes and count to three,
One, two, three!
Open your eyes. What can you see?
Please tell me!
A robot, a robot,
A robot for me!

Close your eyes and count to three,
One, two, three!
Open your eyes. What can you see?
Please tell me!
A game, a game,
A game for me!

Close your eyes and count to three,
One, two, three!
Open your eyes. What can you see?
Please tell me!
A scooter, a scooter,
A scooter for me!

2.2 Tommy's music 4

You're a robot. Play with a ball.
You're a robot. Play on a scooter.
You're a robot. Rock a dolly.
You're a robot. Dance.

2.3 Story 4: *What a mess!*

1.

Narrator: Tommy, Polly and Tina have new toys.
Tommy: Look at my new scooter!
Polly: Look at my new game!
Tina: Look at my new robot.
Robot: Beautiful hair! Beautiful hair! Beautiful hair!

2.

Narrator: Here's Tina's mummy.
Tina's mummy: It's tea time.
Tina: I'm hungry. Come on, Tommy.
Polly: Yummy, yummy. Come on, Tommy.
Tommy: In a minute …

3.

Narrator: What is Tommy doing?
Tommy: Hmm? Five, four, three, two, one. Go robot!

4.

Narrator: Oh no! Look at the robot and the toys! What a mess!
Robot: Teddies! Balls! Dollies! Teddies! Balls! Dollies! Teddies! Balls! Dollies!
Tommy: Stop! Stop!

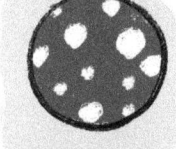

5.

Narrator: Oh no! Look at the robot and the game! What a mess!
Robot: Game! Game! Game!
Tommy: Stop! Stop!

6.

Narrator: Oh no! Look at the robot and the scooter! What a mess!
Robot: Scooter! Scooter! Scooter!
Tommy: Stop! Stop! Stop!

7.

Narrator: Oh no! What a mess!
Polly: Oh no! What a mess!
Tommy: Sorry Tina!
Tina: Don't worry, Tommy. One, two, three, four, five. Go robot!

8.

Robot: Tidy up. Tidy up. Tidy up.
Tommy: Ha, ha, ha! Thank you, Tina.
Tina: You're welcome. Ha, ha, ha!

2.4 Story chant 4: *What a mess!*

The robot has the toys.
What a mess!
Stop! Stop! Stop!

The robot has the game.
What a mess!
Stop! Stop! Stop!

The robot has the scooter.
What a mess!
Stop! Stop! Stop!

2.5 CONTINUOUS ASSESSMENT

Activity 1

Get the Tommy sticker and stick it next to the robot.
Get the Twig sticker and stick it next to the slide.
Get the Polly sticker and stick it next to the dolly.
Get the babies sticker and stick it next to the game.
Get the Petal sticker and stick it next to the bike.
Get the Tina sticker and stick it next to the scooter.

Activity 2

Pick up a pink crayon and trace the 5.
Pick up a yellow crayon and trace the rectangle.
Pick up an orange crayon and trace the 6.
Pick up a green crayon and trace the square.
Pick up a black crayon and trace the 4.

Unit 4 Audio transcripts

3.9 Authentic song 4: One finger one thumb keep moving.

One finger, one thumb.
Keep moving.
One finger, one thumb.
Keep moving.
We'll all be merry and bright.
One finger, one thumb, one arm,
Keep moving.
One finger, one thumb, one arm,
Keep moving.
We'll all be merry and bright.
One finger, one thumb, one arm, one leg,
Keep moving.
One finger, one thumb, one arm, one leg,
Keep moving.
We'll all be merry and bright.
One finger, one thumb, one arm, one leg,
One nod of the head,
Keep moving.
One finger, one thumb, one arm, one leg,
One nod of the head,
Keep moving.
We'll all be merry and bright.

3.10 Photo Poster 4: Pictures in order. Look at the poster. Listen and mime. Listen and repeat.

Hello. My name's Grace. I'm 5. Exercise makes us strong.

This boy's favourite is playing football.
This girl's favourite is jumping on a trampoline.
This boy's favourite is riding a bike.
This girl's favourite is running.
This boy's favourite is dancing.
This girl's favourite is skipping.
This boy's favourite is swimming.

3.11 Photo Poster 4: Pictures not in order. Look at the poster. Listen and mime. Listen and repeat.

Hello. My name's Grace. I'm 5. Exercise makes us strong.

This boy's favourite is dancing.
This boy's favourite is playing football.
This girl's favourite is skipping.
This boy's favourite is riding a bike.
This girl's favourite is jumping on a trampoline.
This boy's favourite is swimming.
This girl's favourite is running.

3.30 Activity Book Unit 4.

Listen and say what's next.
1. swimming   ball   robot   dolly
2. swing   bike   skipping
3. slide   monster
4. skipping   teddy   scooter

Listen and circle what's next with a pencil.
1. swimming   ball   robot   dolly
2. swing   bike   skipping
3. slide   monster
4. skipping   teddy   scooter

Unit 5 Audio transcripts

2.6 Action song 5: *Wake up!*

Wake up! Jump out of bed!
Put your trousers on! (x3)
And your socks and shoes.
And your socks and shoes. Socks and shoes!

Wake up! Jump out of bed!
Put your T-shirt on! (x3)
And your socks and shoes.
And your socks and shoes. Socks and shoes!

Wake up! Jump out of bed!
Put your jumper on! (x3)
And your socks and shoes.
And your socks and shoes. Socks and shoes!

2.7 Tommy's music 5

Put your trousers on slowly.
Put your jumper on quickly.
Put your shoes on slowly.
Put your jacket on quickly.
Now you're ready! Dance to school.

2.8 Story 5: *I'm Tommy's parrot!*

1.

Narrator: It's carnival. Twig is helping Tina.
Twig: Twinkle winkle, twinkle winkle. Twinkle winkle, twinkle, wink! Make a spell and do it well!
One, two, three!

2.

Narrator: Oh! Tina is a fire fighter!
Tina: Look at me! A yellow T-shirt and a yellow hat and yellow shoes and black trousers.
I'm a fire fighter! Yipee!

3.

Narrator: Petal is helping Polly. And Twig is helping Tommy.
Petal & Twig: Twinkle winkle, twinkle winkle. Twinkle winkle, twinkle, wink! Make a spell and do it well! One, two, three!

4.

Narrator: Oh Polly is a princess!
Polly: Look at me! Pink shoes, a pink dress and a pink hat. I'm a princess! Whoopee!
Narrator: And Tommy is a pirate.
Tommy: Look at me! Yellow socks, orange trousers, a green jumper. And a little parrot!
I'm a pirate!! Hurray!

5.

Narrator: Oh dear! Polly isn't happy. She doesn't like Tommy's parrot.
Polly: I'm Tommy's parrot! I don't want that little parrot.

6.

Narrator: Oh dear! Polly is sad! Tommy is sad too.
Polly: Boo hoo! I'm Tommy's parrot!
Tommy: Oh dear! Don't cry Polly!
Narrator: But where's the little parrot?

7.

Narrator: Oh look! There's the little parrot.
He's talking to Polly.
Pirate parrot: What beautiful shoes!!!
What a beautiful dress! What a beautiful hat!
What a beautiful parrot princess!
Polly: Oh! Thank you!

8.

Narrator: Oh look! Everyone is dancing together.
Everyone is happy!
Tina: I like dancing!
Tommy: I like dancing!
Pirate parrot: I like dancing!
Polly: And I like the little parrot!
All: Ha, ha, ha!

2.9 Story chant 5: *I'm Tommy's parrot!*

Tommy is a pirate.
He has a little parrot.
Squawk, squawk, squawk!

Polly is sad.
I'm Tommy's parrot.
Boo hoo hoo!

What a beautiful princess.
Polly is happy now!
Oh! Thank you!

2.10 CONTINUOUS ASSESSMENT

Activity 1

Get the Petal sticker and stick it next to the jacket.
Get the Tommy sticker and stick it next to the socks.
Get the Polly sticker and stick it next to the trousers.
Get the babies sticker and stick it next to the shoes.
Get the Twig sticker and stick it next to the T-shirt.
Get the Tina sticker and stick it next to the jumper.

Activity 2

Pick up a blue crayon trand trace the 5.
Pick up a purple crayon and trace the 7.
Pick up a brown crayon and trace the 6.
Pick up a yellow crayon and colour the spider on the hat.
Pick up a red crayon and colour the spider under the hat.

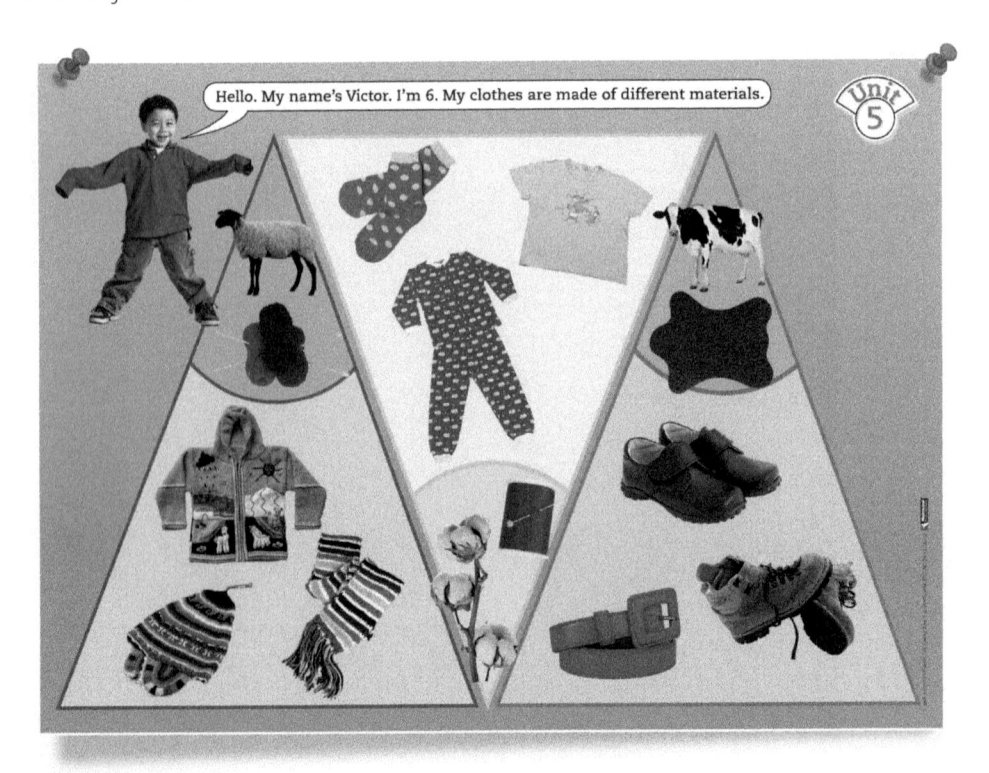

Unit 5   Audio transcripts

3.12 Authentic song 5: She'll be coming round the mountain.

She'll be coming round the mountain,
When she comes.
She'll be coming round the mountain,
When she comes.
She'll be coming round the mountain,
Coming round the mountain,
Coming round the mountain when she comes.

Singing I, I yippie, yippie I,
Singing I, I yippie, yippie I,
Singing I, I yippie, I, I yippie,
I, I yippie, yippie I.

She'll be riding a white horse when she comes.
She'll be riding a white horse when she comes.
She'll be riding a white horse, riding a white horse,
Riding a white horse when she comes.

She'll be wearing pink pyjamas when she comes.
She'll be wearing pink pyjamas when she comes.
She'll be wearing pink pyjamas, wearing pink pyjamas,
Wearing pink pyjamas when she comes.

3.13 Photo Poster 5: Pictures in order. Look at the poster. Listen and mime. Listen and repeat.

Hello. My name's Victor. I'm 6.
My clothes are made of different materials.

Victor's jumper is made of wool.
Victor's scarf is made of wool.
Victor's hat is made of wool.
Victor's pyjamas are made of cotton.
Victor's T-shirt is made of cotton.
Victor's socks are made of cotton.
Victor's shoes are made of leather.
Victor's boots are made of leather.
Victor's belt is made of leather.

3.14 Photo Poster 5: Pictures not in order. Look at the poster. Listen and mime. Listen and repeat.

Hello. My name's Victor. I'm 6.
My clothes are made of different materials.

Victor's pyjamas are made of cotton.
Victor's hat is made of wool.
Victor's boots are made of leather.
Victor's T-shirt is made of cotton.
Victor's scarf is made of wool.
Victor's shoes are made of leather.
Victor's jumper is made of wool.
Victor's belt is made of leather.
Victor's socks are made of cotton.

3.31 Activity Book Unit 5.

Listen and say what's next.
1. hat   leather   T-shirt   jumper
2. dress   pyjamas   jacket
3. shoes   scarf
4. socks   boots   wool

Listen and circle what's next with a pencil.
1. hat   leather   T-shirt   jumper
2. dress   pyjamas   jacket
3. shoes   scarf
4. socks   boots   wool

Unit 6   Audio transcripts

2.11   Action song 6: *We're off*

We're off. We're off. We're off to go to school.
Get in the car. Close the door. Put your seat belt on.
Clunk click!
Go straight on. Go round the corner. Go straight on again.
There's the school. Put on your brake. Stop!
We're at the school.

We're off. We're off. We're off to go to a shop.
Get in the car. Close the door. Put your seat belt on.
Clunk click!
Go straight on. Go round the corner. Go straight on again.
There's the shop. Put on your brake. Stop!
We're at the shop.

We're off. We're off. We're off to the hospital.
Get in the car. Close the door. Put your seat belt on.
Clunk click!
Go straight on. Go round the corner. Go straight on again.
There's the hospital. Put on your brake. Stop!
We're at the hospital.

2.12   Tommy's music 6

Go to a shop and buy a ball.
Bounce your ball.
Go to a shop and buy some crayons.
Colour with your crayons.
Go to a shop and buy a car.
Put your seat belt on and drive your car.

2.13   Story 6: *Tommy's a wonderful tiger!*

1.

Narrator: Tommy and Tina and Polly are playing hospital. Tommy is the doctor. Oh dear!
Tina: Tommy! I can't see!
Polly: Tommy! I can't walk! Ah! Ouch!
Tommy: Oops! I'm not good at playing hospital!

2.

Narrator: Tommy and Tina and Polly are playing school. Tommy is the teacher. He's reading a book. Oh dear!
Tommy: Hmm! Hmm! This is a very difficult book!
Tina: Tommy! The book is upside down!
Tommy: Oops! I'm not good at playing school!

3.

Narrator: Tommy and Tina and Polly are playing shop. Oh dear!
Tina: Atishoo! Oh I'm white!
Polly: Atishoo! Oh I'm white!
Tommy: Oops! I'm not good at playing shop!

4.

Narrator: Tommy is sad.
Tommy: I'm not good at playing hospital or school or shop.

Tina: Hmmm ... Let's go and play outside!
Polly: Yes! That's a good idea!

5.

Narrator: Tommy is running.
Polly: Look at Tommy.
Tina: Run, run, run Tommy!

6.

Narrator: Tommy is jumping.
Polly: Look at Tommy.
Tina: Jump, jump, jump Tommy!

7.

Narrator: Tommy's swimming.
Polly: Look at Tommy!
Tina: Swim, swim, swim Tommy!

8.

Narrator: Tommy isn't good at playing hospital or school or shop but he's a wonderful tiger!
Tina: Tommy you're a wonderful tiger!
Polly: Tommy you're a wonderful tiger!
Tommy: Thank you everyone! Woo!
All: Ha, ha!

2.14   Story chant 6: *Tommy's a wonderful tiger!*

Look at Tommy running!
Run, run, run!

Look at Tommy jumping!
Jump, jump, jump!

Look at Tommy swimming!
Swim, swim, swim!

Tommy's a wonderful tiger!
Thank you everyone!

2.15   CONTINUOUS ASSESSMENT

Activity 1

Get the Tommy sticker and stick it next to the school.
Get the babies sticker and stick it next to the fire fighter.
Get the Tina sticker and stick it next to the train.
Get the Twig sticker and stick it next to the hospital.
Get the Polly sticker and stick it next to the police officer.
Get the Petal sticker and stick it next to the shop.

Activity 2

Pick up a black crayon trand trace the 8.
Pick up a yellow crayon and trace the 6.
Pick up a blue crayon and trace the 7.
Pick up a green crayon and colour the loud baby.
Pick up a red crayon and colour the quiet baby.

Unit 6   Audio transcripts

3.15   Authentic song 6: The wheels on the bus.

The wheels on the bus go round and round,
Round and round,
Round and round.
The wheels on the bus go round and round all day long.

The wipers on the bus go swish, swish, swish…

The bell on the bus goes ring, ring, ring…

The horn on the bus goes toot, toot, toot…

Then at night the bus goes to sleep,
Goes to sleep, goes to sleep.
Then at night the bus goes to sleep all night long.

3.16   Photo Poster 6: Pictures in order. Look at the poster. Listen and mime. Listen and repeat.

Hello. My name's Daisy. I'm 5.
Look what happens when you post a letter.

The boy posts the letter in a post box.
The letter goes by van.
Machines sort the letters.
The letter goes by lorry,
By boat,
By plane or…
By train.
At the post office a postman puts the letter in a bag.
A postman takes the letter by bike,
By scooter or on foot.
A postman puts the letter in the letter box.

3.17   Photo Poster 6: Pictures not in order. Look at the poster. Listen and mime. Listen and repeat.

Hello. My name's Daisy. I'm 5.
Look what happens when you post a letter.

A postman takes the letter by bike,
By scooter or on foot.
The boy posts the letter in a post box.
A postman puts the letter in the letter box.
At the post office a postman puts the letter in a bag.
The letter goes by lorry,
By boat,
By plane or…
By train.
The letter goes by van.
Machines sort the letters.

3.32   Activity Book Unit 6.

Listen and say what's next.
1. doctor   bus   postbox
2. shop   postman
3. hospital   fire fighter   car
4. school   post office   plane   police officer

Listen and circle what's next with a pencil.
1. doctor   bus   postbox
2. shop   postman
3. hospital   fire fighter   car
4. school   post office   plane   police officer

Unit 7   Audio transcripts

2.16   Action song 7: *Three big pizzas*

Three big pizzas in the pizza shop,
With tomato and ham and cheese on top.
Along comes Tommy with a euro to pay,
Buys a big pizza and takes it away!

Two big pizzas in the pizza shop,
With tomato and ham and cheese on top.
Along comes Tina with a euro to pay,
Buys a big pizza and takes it away!

One big pizza in the pizza shop,
With tomato and ham and cheese on top.
Along comes Polly with a euro to pay,
Buys a big pizza and takes it away!

No pizzas left!

2.17   Tommy's music 7

Put some cheese on your pizza.
Put some ham on your pizza.
Put some tomato on your pizza.
Eat your pizza, yummy!
Dance.

2.18   Story 7: *Wash your hands, please!*

1.

Narrator: Look! Here's mummy and here's Tommy's brother Ted and the baby tigers. They are washing their hands. Here's Tommy. Tommy isn't washing his hands!
Mummy: Wash your hands before breakfast please.
Ted: I'm washing my hands.
Baby tigers: We're washing our hands.
Tommy: I don't want to wash my hands.
Narrator: Naughty Tommy!

2.

Narrator: The children are eating breakfast.
Tommy: Yummy! Yummy! Biscuits and yoghurt!
Ted: Yummy! Yummy! Biscuits and yoghurt!
Babies: Yummy! Yummy! Biscuits and yoghurt!

3.

Narrator: Tommy is at school. It's time for the morning snack.
Teacher: Wash your hands before the morning snack, please.
Polly: I'm washing my hands.
Tina: I'm washing my hands.
Tommy: I don't want to wash my hands.
Teacher: Naughty Tommy.

4.

Narrator: Tommy and Polly and Tina are eating the morning snack.

Tommy: Yummy! Yummy! A ham sandwich!
Tina: Yummy! Yummy! A tomato sandwich!
Polly: Yummy! Yummy! A cheese sandwich!

5.

Narrator: Oh dear! Tommy's tummy hurts!
Tommy: Ooh. My tummy hurts!

6.

Polly: What's the matter Tommy?
Tommy: My tummy hurts!
Teacher: You must wash your hands, Tommy!

7.

Narrator: It's time for lunch.
Teacher: Wash your hands before lunch please.
Tommy: Me first!

8.

Narrator: Oh dear! What IS Tommy doing now?
Teacher: Just wash your hands Tommy.
Tina & Polly: Tommy!
Tommy: Oops!

2.19   Story chant 7: *Wash your hands, please!*

Wash your hands,
Before breakfast.
Splash, splash, splash!

Wash your hands,
Before the morning snack.
Splash, splash, splash!

Wash your hands,
Before lunch.
Splash, splash, splash!

Just your hands, Tommy!

2.20   CONTINUOUS ASSESSMENT

Activity 1

Get the Petal sticker and stick it next to the ham.
Get the Twig sticker and stick it next to the yoghurt.
Get the Tina sticker and stick it next to the cheese.
Get the babies sticker and stick it next to the banana.
Get the Tommy sticker and stick it next to the biscuit.
Get the Polly sticker and stick it next to the tomato.

Activity 2

Pick up a pink crayon and trace the 8.
Pick up an orange crayon and trace the 7.
Pick up a brown crayon and trace the 9.
Pick up a yellow crayon and colour the spider in the box.
Pick up a black crayon and colour the spider next to the box.

Unit 7   Audio transcripts

3.18 Authentic song 7: Today is Monday.

It's dinner time!

Today is Monday.
Monday green beans.
All you hungry children,
Come and eat it up!

Today is Tuesday.
Tuesday spaghetti.
Monday green beans.
All you hungry children,
Come and eat it up!

Today is Wednesday.
Wednesday soup.
Tuesday spaghetti.
Monday green beans.
All you hungry children,
Come and eat it up!

Today is Thursday.
Thursday fish.
Wednesday soup.
Tuesday spaghetti.
Monday green beans.
All you hungry children,
Come and eat it up!

Today is Friday.
Friday pizza.
Thursday fish.
Wednesday soup.
Tuesday spaghetti.
Monday green beans.
All you hungry children,
Come and eat it up!

Today is Saturday.
Saturday chicken.
Friday pizza.
Thursday fish.
Wednesday soup.
Tuesday spaghetti.
Monday green beans.
All you hungry children,
Come and eat it up!

Today is Sunday.
Sunday ice cream.
Saturday chicken.
Friday pizza.
Thursday fish.
Wednesday soup.
Tuesday spaghetti.
Monday green beans.
All you hungry children,
Come and eat it up!

3.19 Poster script 7.

Hello. My name's Harry. I'm 6. Are your snacks healthy?

Fruit is good for you.
Yoghurt is good for you.
A sandwich is good for you.
Nuts are good for you.
Carrots are good for you.
Cheese is good for you.
Sweets are not good for you.
Crisps are not good for you.
Buns are not good for you.
Cakes are not good for you.

3.20 Photo Poster 7: Pictures not in order. Look at the poster. Listen and mime. Listen and repeat.

Hello. My name's Harry. I'm 6. Are your snacks healthy?

Sweets are not good for you.
Nuts are good for you.
Cheese is good for you.
Buns are not good for you.
Yoghurt is good for you.
A sandwich is good for you.
Crisps are not good for you.
Fruit is good for you.
Cakes are not good for you.
Carrots are good for you.

3.33 Activity Book Unit 7.

Listen and say what's next.
1. cheese   cherry   apple
2. potato   yoghurt   tomato   egg
3. sandwich   orange
4. biscuit   green bean   pear

Listen and circle what's next with a pencil.
1. cheese   cherry   apple
2. potato   yoghurt   tomato   egg
3. sandwich   orange
4. biscuit   green bean   pear

Unit 8   Audio transcripts

2.21   Action song 8: *Roll over!*

There are 6 in the bed and Tommy says,
"Roll over! Roll over!".
So they all roll over and Sheep falls out.
There are 5 in the bed … Dog
There are 4 in the bed … Lion
There are 3 in the bed … Bear
There are 2 in the bed … Monkey
There's one in the bed and Tommy says,
"Oops sorry everyone! Come back to bed!"

2.22   Tommy's music 8

Sleep like a bear.
Kiss like a lion.
Dance like a monkey.
Sleep like a lion.
Kiss like a monkey.
Dance like a bear.

2.23   Story 8: *I'm sad! I'm grumpy! I'm sleepy!*

1.

Narrator: Tommy sees a monkey. The monkey is sad!
Tommy: Hello monkey. How are you?
Monkey: I'm sad!
Tommy: What's the matter?

2.

Narrator: The monkey doesn't like her hair!
Monkey: Look! My sister's hair is straight but my hair is curly! I don't want curly hair! Boo hoo!
Tommy: Oh dear! Come with me.

3.

Narrator: Tommy and the monkey see a lion. The lion is grumpy!
Tommy: Hello lion. How are you?
Lion: I'm grumpy!
Monkey: What's the matter?

4.

Narrator: The lion is little.
Lion: Look! My sister is big but I'm little! I don't want to be little! Grrrr!
Tommy: Oh dear! Come with me.

5.

Narrator: Tommy and the lion and the monkey meet a bear. The bear is sleepy!
Tommy: Hello bear. How are you?
Bear: I'm sleepy!
Lion: What's the matter?

6.

Narrator: The bear has a baby brother.
Bear: My baby brother cries all day and all night! I can't sleep!
Baby brother: Waa!
Tommy: Oh dear! Come with me.

7.

Narrator: Tommy and the lion and the monkey and the bear meet Petal and Twig. Petal and Twig are thinking.
Tommy: What's the matter Petal?
Petal: We want to do some magic but we need a sad monkey, a grumpy lion and a sleepy bear.
Monkey: I'm sad!
Lion: I'm grumpy!
Bear: I'm sleepy!
Twig: Oh good! Here we go then.
Twinkle winkle, twinkle winkle.
Twinkle winkle, twinkle, wink!
Make a spell and do it well! One, two, three!

8.

Narrator: Look! The magic makes space hoppers for everyone!
Petal: Thank you everyone.
Monkey: Now I'm not sad!
Lion: Now I'm not grumpy!
Bear: Now I'm not sleepy!
Narrator: In fact, everyone is very happy!

2.24   Story chant 8: *I'm sad! I'm grumpy! I'm sleepy!*

I'm a sad, sad monkey!
I'm a grumpy, grumpy lion!
I'm a sleepy, sleepy bear!

We need a sad monkey.
We need a grumpy lion.
We need a sleepy bear.

Boing, boing, boing! Now everyone is happy!

2.25   CONTINUOUS ASSESSMENT

Activity 1

Get the Tina sticker and stick it next to the bear.
Get the Petal sticker and stick it next to the cow.
Get the Twig sticker and stick it next to the dog.
Get the Tommy sticker and stick it next to the monkey.
Get the Polly sticker and stick it next to the sheep.
Get the babies sticker and stick it next to the lion.

Activity 2

Pick up a green crayon and trace the 8.
Pick up a red crayon and trace the 10.
Pick up a purple crayon and trace the 9.
Pick up an orange crayon and colour the spider in front of the bear.
Pick up a yellow crayon and colour the spider behind the bear.

Unit 8   Audio transcripts

3.21 Authentic song 8: There was an old lady who swallowed a fly.

There was an old lady who swallowed a fly.
I don't know why she swallowed a fly,
Oh why, oh why?

There was an old lady who swallowed a spider.
It wiggled and wiggled and tickled inside her.
She swallowed the spider to catch the fly.
I don't know why she swallowed a fly,
Oh why, oh why ?

There was an old lady who swallowed a bird.
She swallowed the bird to catch the spider
That wiggled and wiggled and tickled inside her.
She swallowed the spider to catch the fly.
I don't know why she swallowed a fly,
Oh why, oh why?

There was an old lady who swallowed a cat.
She swallowed the cat to catch the bird.
She swallowed the bird to catch the spider,
That wiggled and wiggled and tickled inside her.
She swallowed the spider to catch the fly.
I don't know why she swallowed a fly,
Oh why, oh why?

There was an old lady who swallowed a dog.
She swallowed the dog to catch the cat.
She swallowed the cat to catch the bird.
She swallowed the bird to catch the spider,
That wiggled and wiggled and tickled inside her.
She swallowed the spider to catch the fly.
I don't know why she swallowed a fly,
Oh why, oh why?

Atchoooooooo…!
Out came the dog, the cat, the bird, the spider,
And the fly… Goodbye.
Goodbye fly.

3.22 Photo Poster 8: Pictures in order. Look at the poster. Listen and mime. Listen and repeat.

Hello. My name's Fatima. I'm 6. I like creepy crawlies.

A beetle has 6 legs.
A spider has 8 legs
A centipede has lots of legs.
A fly has little wings.
A butterfly has big wings.
A bee is yellow and black.
A ladybird is red with black spots.
A mosquito is very little.

3.23 Photo Poster 8: Pictures not in order. Look at the poster. Listen and mime. Listen and repeat.

Hello. My name's Fatima. I'm 6. I like creepy crawlies.

A fly has little wings.
A ladybird is red with black spots.
A mosquito is very little.
A spider has 8 legs.
A bee is yellow and black.
A centipede has lots of legs.
A butterfly has big wings.
A beetle has 6 legs.

3.34 Activity Book Unit 8.

Listen and say what's next.
1. fish   chicken   spider
2. ladybird   tiger   dog   cow
3. sheep   fly   cat
4. elephant   monkey

Listen and circle what's next with a pencil.
1. fish   chicken   spider
2. ladybird   tiger   dog   cow
3. sheep   fly   cat
4. elephant   monkey

Unit 9 Audio transcripts

2.26 Action song 9: *Flying high*

Flying high,
Flying low.
Flying round and round,
We go!

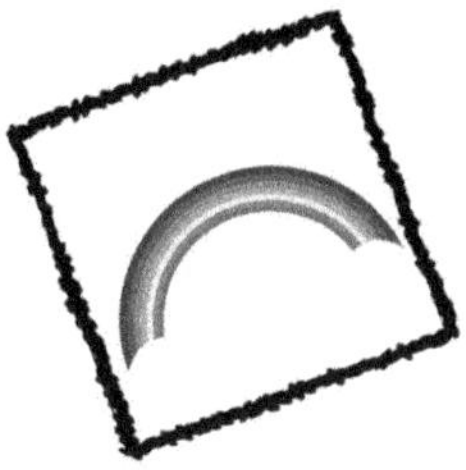

Jump over a rainbow,
Dance on a star.
Draw a smile on the moon,
Stop where you are.

Flying high,
Flying low.
Flying round and round,
We go!

2.27 Tommy's music 9

Draw a rainbow.
Draw a star.
Draw a moon.
Jump over a rainbow.
Dance on a star.
Draw a smile on the moon and hug it.

2.28 Story 9: *Magic sky*

1.

Narrator: Look! Twig and Petal are on their magic carpet!
Petal: Hello Tommy. Come for a ride!
Tommy: Hello. Where are we going?
Twig: Surprise!

2.

Narrator: Look!
Tommy: It's a rainbow!
Petal: Ha, ha! Yes, it's a rainbow.

3.

Petal: Catch the rainbow, Tommy.
Twig: And put it in my bag.
Tommy: OK.

4.

Narrator: Look!
Petal: Catch a star, Tommy.
Twig: And put it in my bag.
Tommy: OK.

5.

Narrator: Look!
Petal: Catch the moon, Tommy.
Twig: And put it in my bag.
Tommy: OK.

6.

Narrator: Tommy is showing Polly and Tina the bag.
Tommy: There's a moon and a rainbow and a star in this bag.
Polly: Ooh!
Tina: Open it!

7.

Narrator: Tommy opens the bag and …
Look at the rainbow and the star and the moon!
Tommy: Come here star! Ouch! Naughty star!
Polly: Come here rainbow!
Tina: Come here moon!

8.

Polly: What does it say?
Tina: It says "Goodbye".
Tommy: Goodbye everyone!

2.29 Story chant 9: *Magic sky*

Catch a rainbow Tommy,
And put it in my bag.
Catch a star Tommy,
And put it in my bag.
Catch the moon Tommy,
And put it in my bag.

A rainbow, a star
and the moon,
All in my bag!

2.30 CONTINUOUS ASSESSMENT

Activity 1

Get the Polly sticker and stick it next to the rainbow.
Get the babies sticker and stick it next to the flower.
Get the Twig sticker and stick it next to the river.
Get the Petal sticker and stick it next to the star.
Get the Tommy sticker and stick it next to the moon.
Get the Tina sticker and stick it next to the sun.

Activity 2

Pick up a pink crayon and trace the circle.
Pick up a black crayon and trace the square.
Pick up a green crayon and trace the triangle.
Pick up a blue crayon and trace the rectangle.
Draw a spider on the circle.
Draw a spider in the square.
Draw a spider under the rectangle.
Draw a spider next to the triangle.

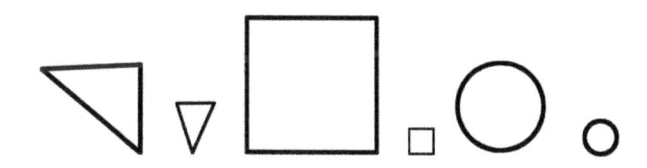

Unit 9 Audio transcripts

3.24 Authentic song 9: I can sing a rainbow. (Children)

Red and orange and yellow and green,
Violet and purple and blue.
I can sing a rainbow,
Sing a rainbow,
Sing a rainbow too.

Look with your eyes,
Listen with your ears,
and sing everything you see,
I can sing a rainbow,
Sing a rainbow,
Sing along with me.

Red and orange and yellow and green,
Violet and purple and blue.
I can sing a rainbow,
Sing a rainbow,
Sing a rainbow too!

3.25 Photo Poster 9: Look at the poster. Listen and mime. Listen and repeat.

Hello. My name's Joe. I'm 5.
Look at the day sky and the night sky.

In the day sky… You can see the sun.
You can see clouds.
You can see planes.
You can see birds.
You can see a rainbow.
In the night sky… You can see stars.
You can see the moon.
You can see fireworks.
You can see bats.
You can see owls.

3.26 Photo Poster 9: Pictures not in order Look at the poster. Listen and mime. Listen and repeat.

Hello. My name's Joe. I'm 5.
Look at the day sky and the night sky.

You can see clouds.
You can see bats.
You can see a rainbow.
You can see fireworks.
You can see birds.
You can see the sun.
You can see owls.
You can see planes.
You can see stars.
You can see the moon.

3.35 Activity Book Unit 9.

Listen and say what's next.
1. rainbow   tree   river   flower
2. beach   sun   sea
3. mountain   moon
4. owl   day   star

Listen and circle what's next with a pencil.
1. rainbow   tree   river   flower
2. beach   sun   sea
3. mountain   moon
4. owl   day   star

1.1

Name: _____

- Find five differences and colour them in picture 2.

1.2

Name: _____

★ Trace the shapes. Colour the circle yellow and the square green. Find the shapes in the picture and colour them the same colour.

1.3

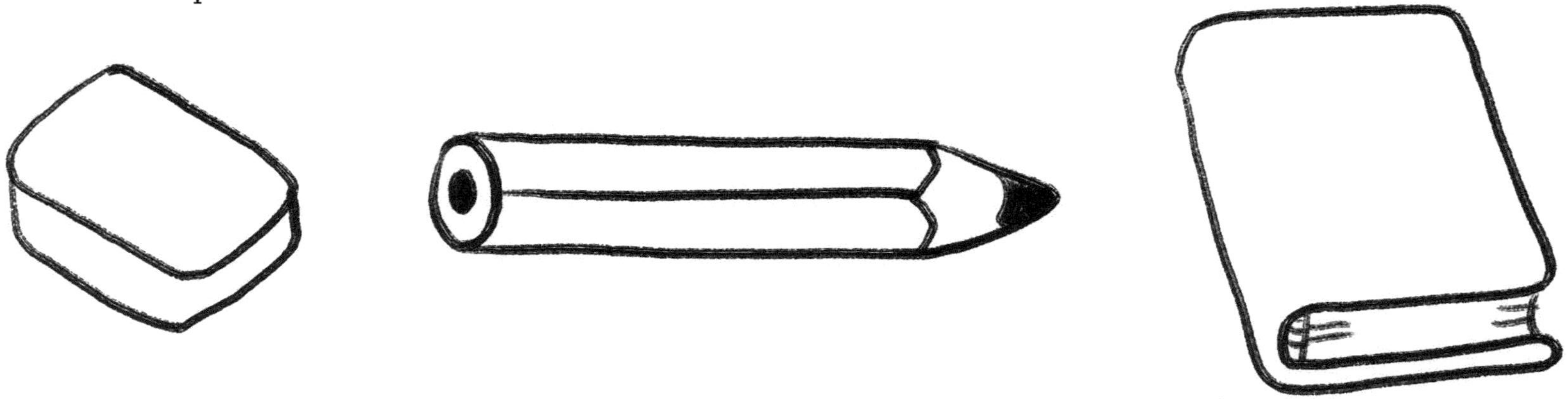

Name: _____

★ Colour the rubber yellow, the pencil red and the book blue.
Then colour the other pictures the same colours.

1.4

Name: _____

- Listen and trace the numbers and shapes with the correct colours.

- Listen and place the stickers.

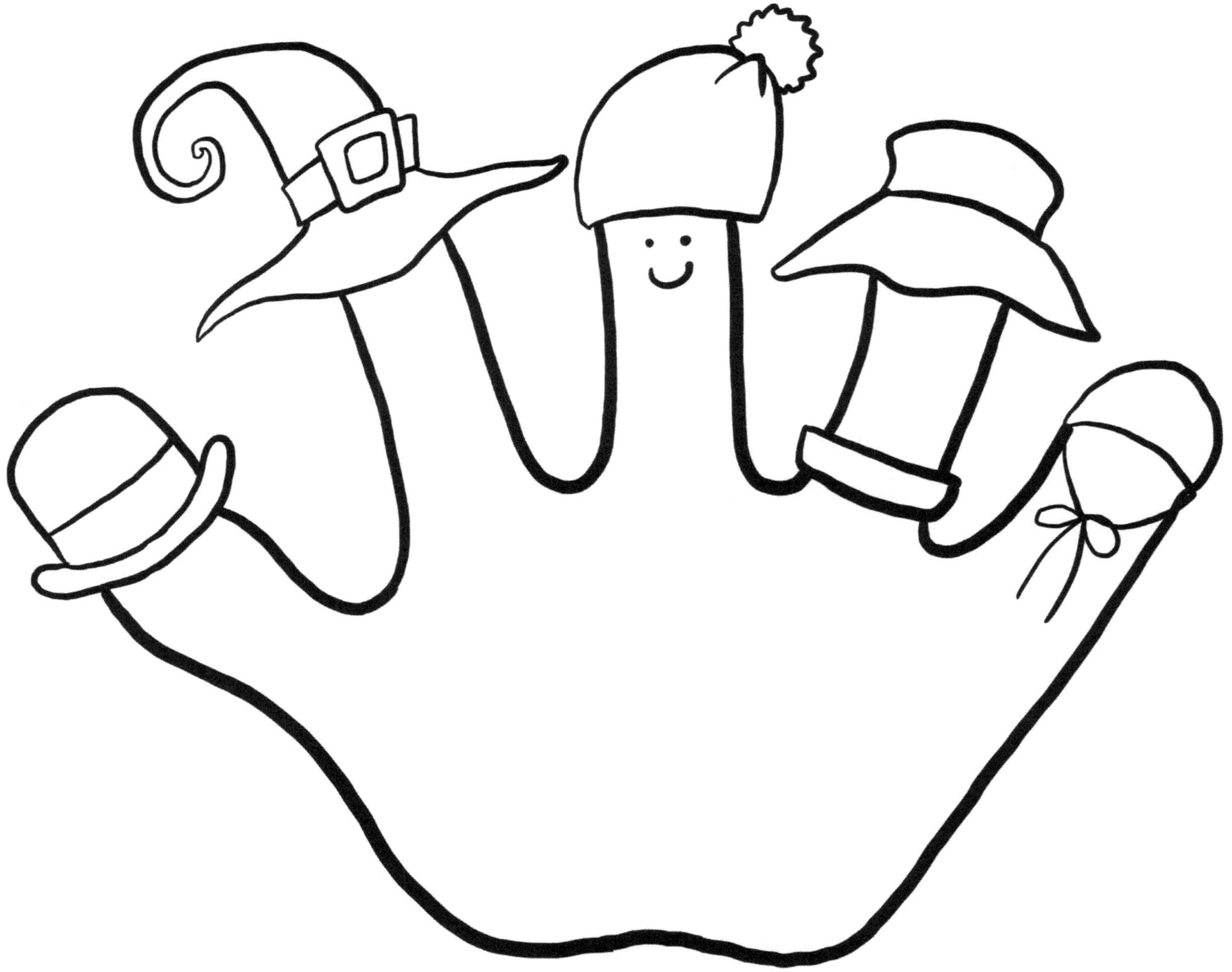

Name: _____

- Colour the hand pink. Draw faces on the fingers.
- Colour each hat a different colour.

Name: _____

- Colour the faces with different colours.
  Trace the frames according to the key.

1.6

2.1

Name: _____

- Trace each line with a different colour.
Continue the lines to what each person is going to take with them.

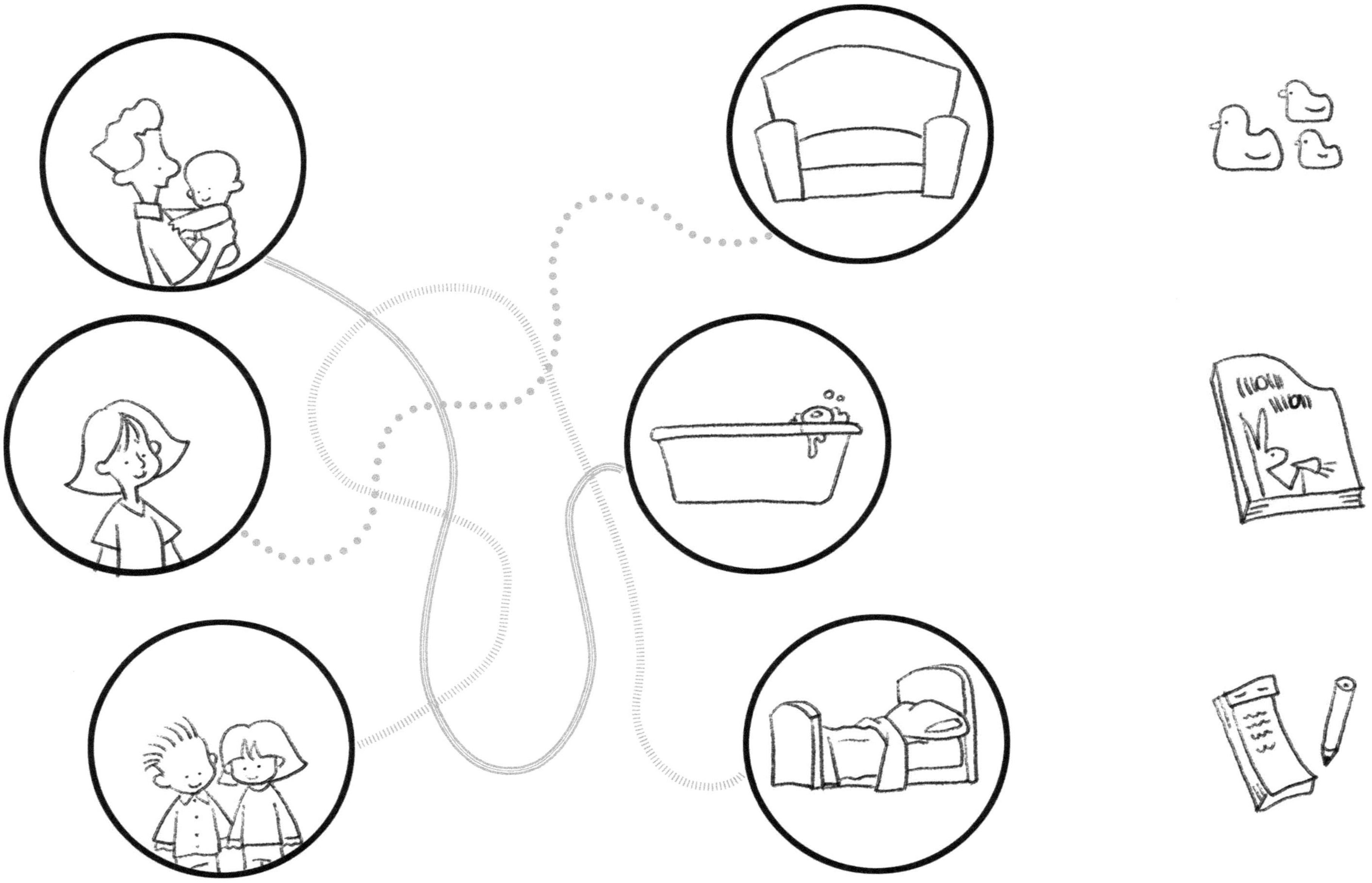

2.2

Name: _____

★ Count the objects in the balloons and write the numbers in the baskets.

3   4   5

2.3

Name: _____

★ Draw lines to match the same family groups.

2.4

Name: _____

★ Listen and trace the numbers and shapes with the correct colours.

★ Listen and place the stickers.

Name: _____

* Roll up pieces of tissue paper and glue them onto the duck: blue for the eyes, orange for the beak and feet, and yellow for the body.

2.6

Name: _____

 Draw what's missing in each of the pictures.

3.1

Name: _____

- Match the parts of the body with the objects.

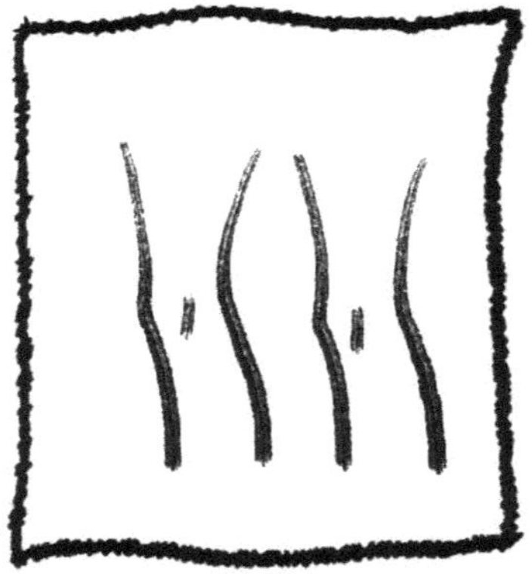

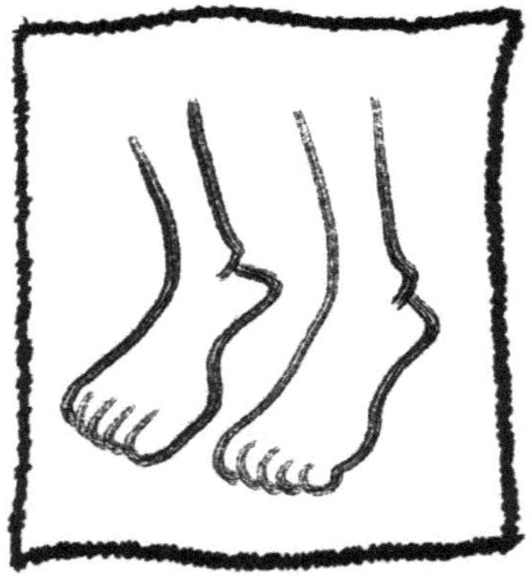

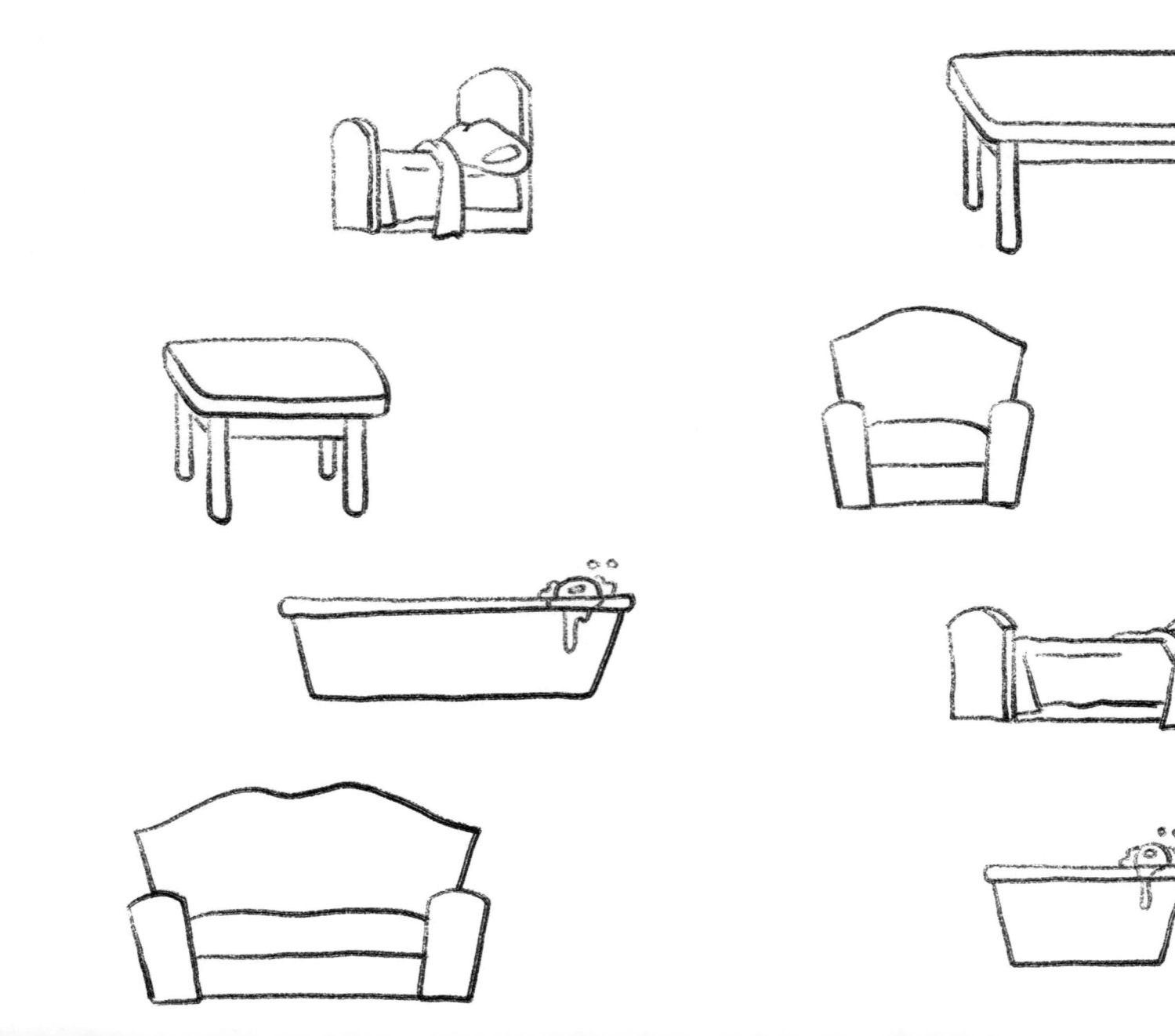

Name: _____

3.2

★ Colour the short objects.

3.3

Name: _____

- Draw the missing body parts on the Christmas trees.

3.4

Name: _____

★ Listen and trace the hair with the correct colours.

★ Listen and place the stickers.

Name: _____

Colour the cymbals on the tambourine. Punch the central part out and stick a piece of tracing paper over the back.

3.6

Name: _____

Circle the Christmas things.

4.1

Name: _____

Count the toys and write the number.

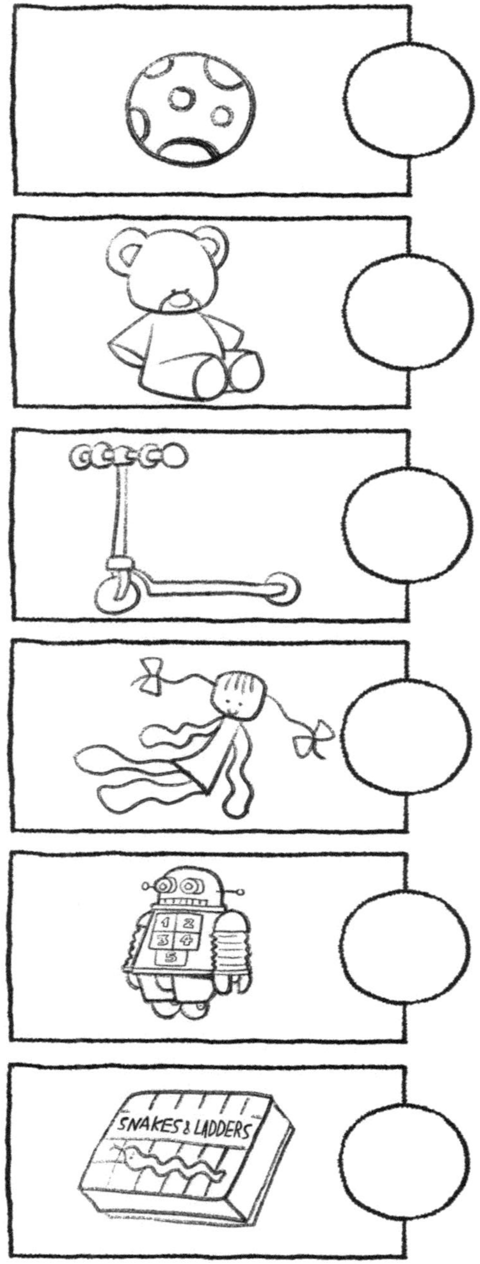

4.2

Name: _____

🍁 Trace the shapes and colour the square pink,
the rectangle orange, the triangle purple and the circle brown.
Colour the robot using the key.

4.3

Name: _____

★ Colour the same toys the same colour.

4.4

Name: _____

* Listen and trace the numbers and shapes with the correct colours.

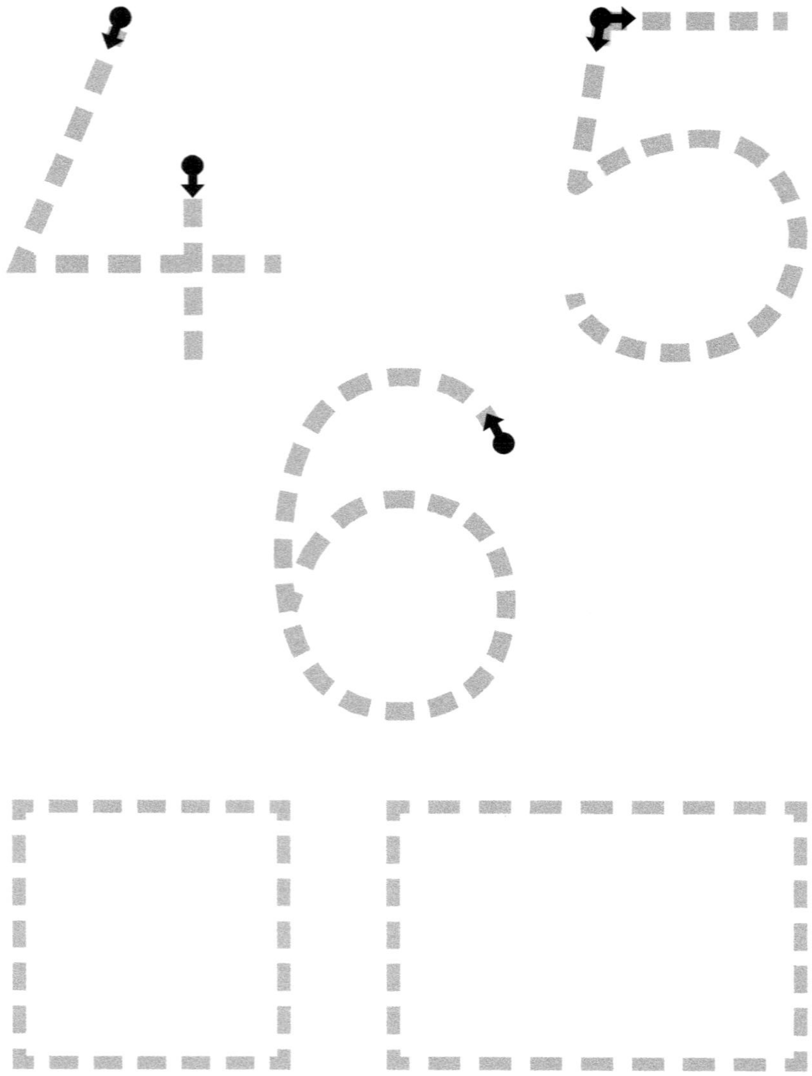

* Listen and place the stickers.

4.5

Name: _____

🌸 Draw your face and hair. Colour the clothes your favourite colours.

4.6

Name: _____

★ Colour the three activities you like best.

5.1

Name: _____

- Colour the odd one out in each line.

5.2

Name: _____

◆ Count the dots and write the number in the first circle. Draw more dots to make seven and write the number in the second circle.

7

5.3

Name: _____

- Draw lines from the clothes to the character that wears them in the story.

Name: _____

5.4

★ Listen and trace the numbers with the correct colours. Listen and colour the spiders with the correct colours.

★ Listen and place the stickers.

5.5

Name: _____

- Colour the pyjamas with a crayon.
- Glue pieces of crepe paper on the horse.

5.6

Name: _____

* Circle the pictures using the following code:

| **red** if they are associated with wool | **green** if they are associated with cotton | **brown** if they are associated with leather. |

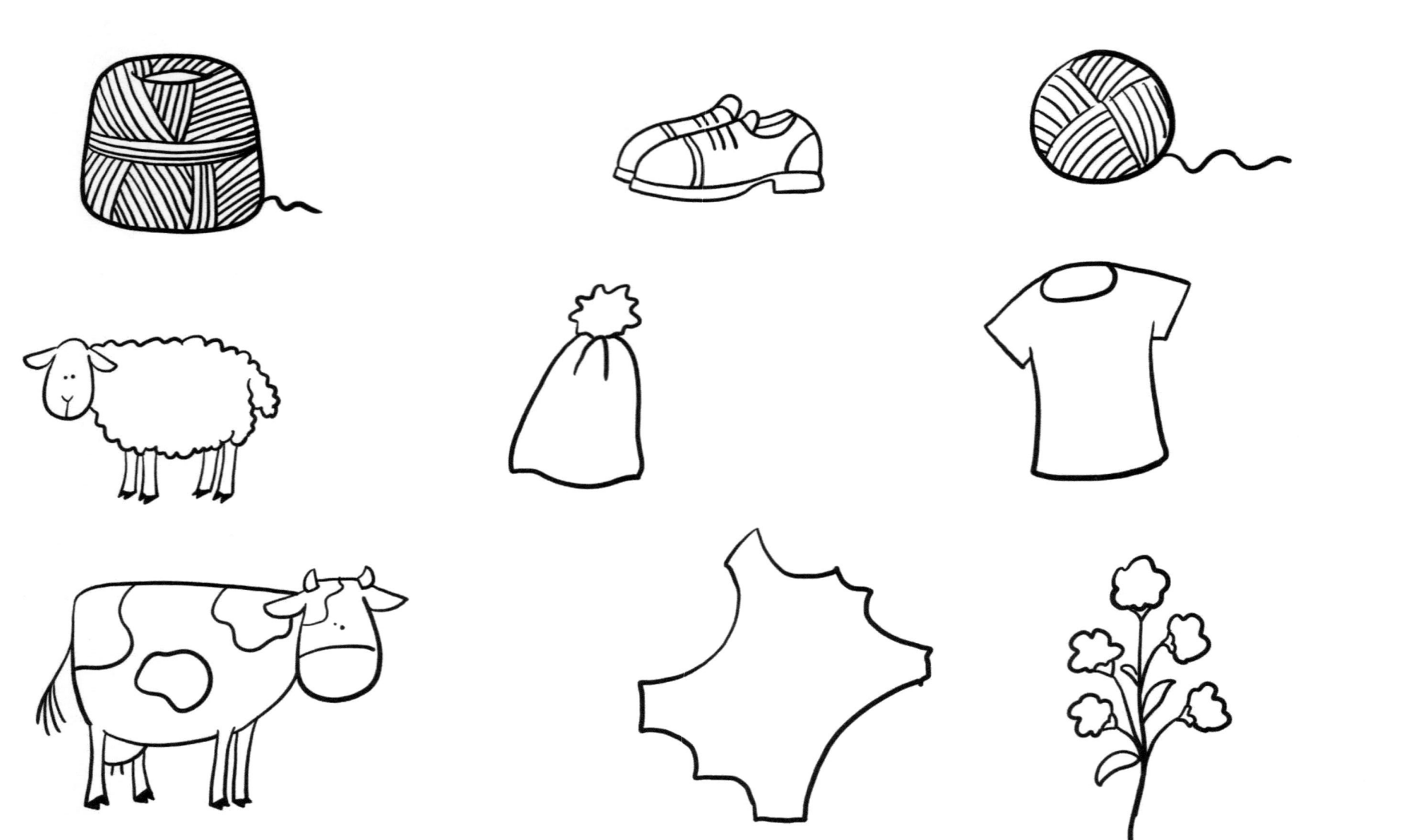

6.1

Name: _____

★ Put gomets on the paths between the people, the transport and the places.

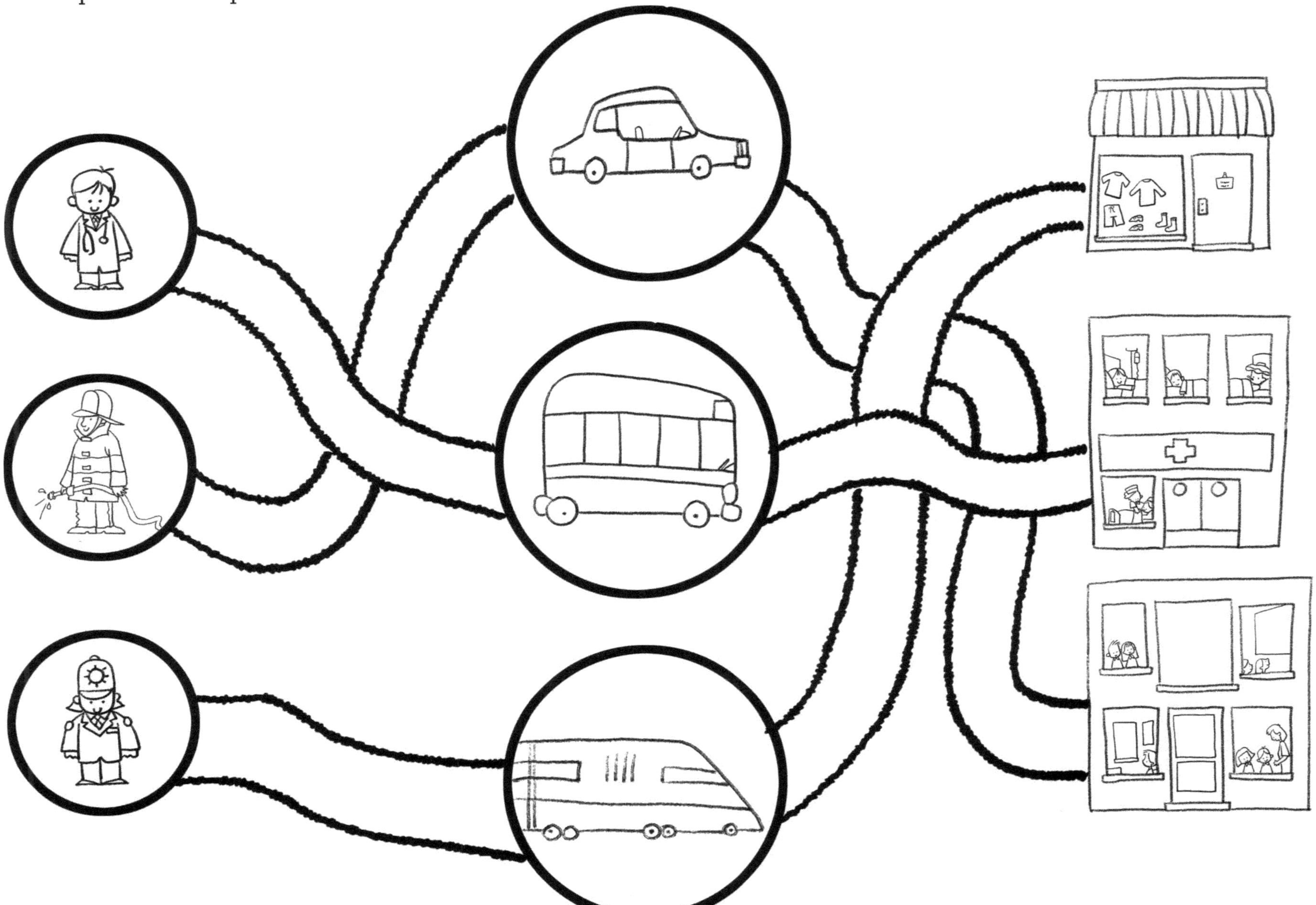

6.2

Name: _____

★ Find eight hidden objects and colour them.

Trace the number eight.

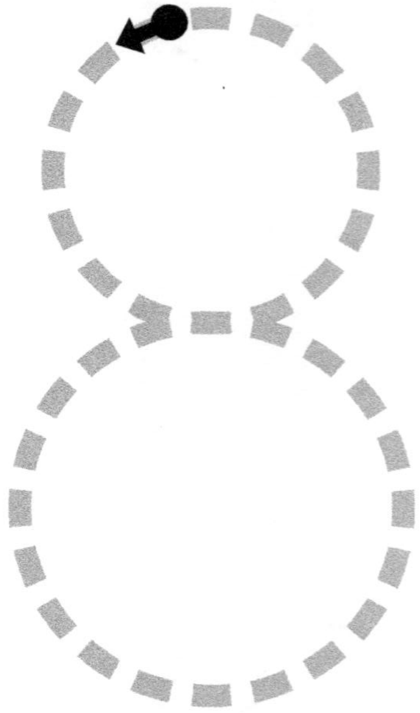

6.3

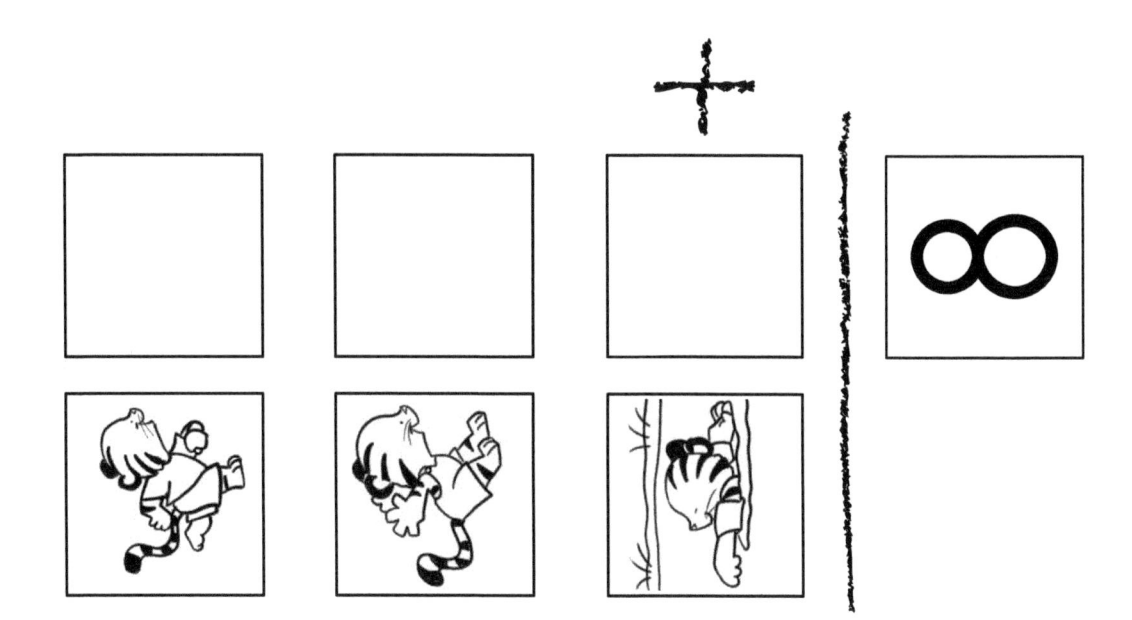

Name: _____

★ Colour the tigers using a different colour for each action and then count them.

| | | | = 8 |

6.4

Name: _____

★ Listen and trace the numbers with the correct colours. Listen and colour the babies the correct colours.

★ Listen and place the stickers.

6.5

Name: _____

🟊 Colour the bus. Press black plasticine onto the wheels. Draw a driver and children in the windows.

Count the postmen.

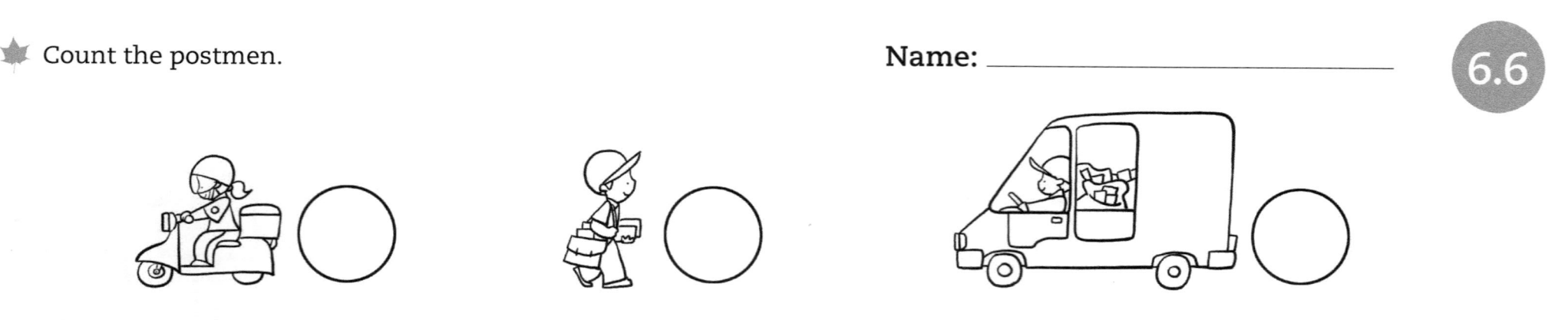

Name: _____

6.6

7.1

Find the differences and colour them in picture 2.

7.2

Name: _____

- Draw a dot either in or next to the box, depending on whether the food is in or next to the basket.

7.3

Name: _____

★ Follow the paths and draw what each person collects in their basket.

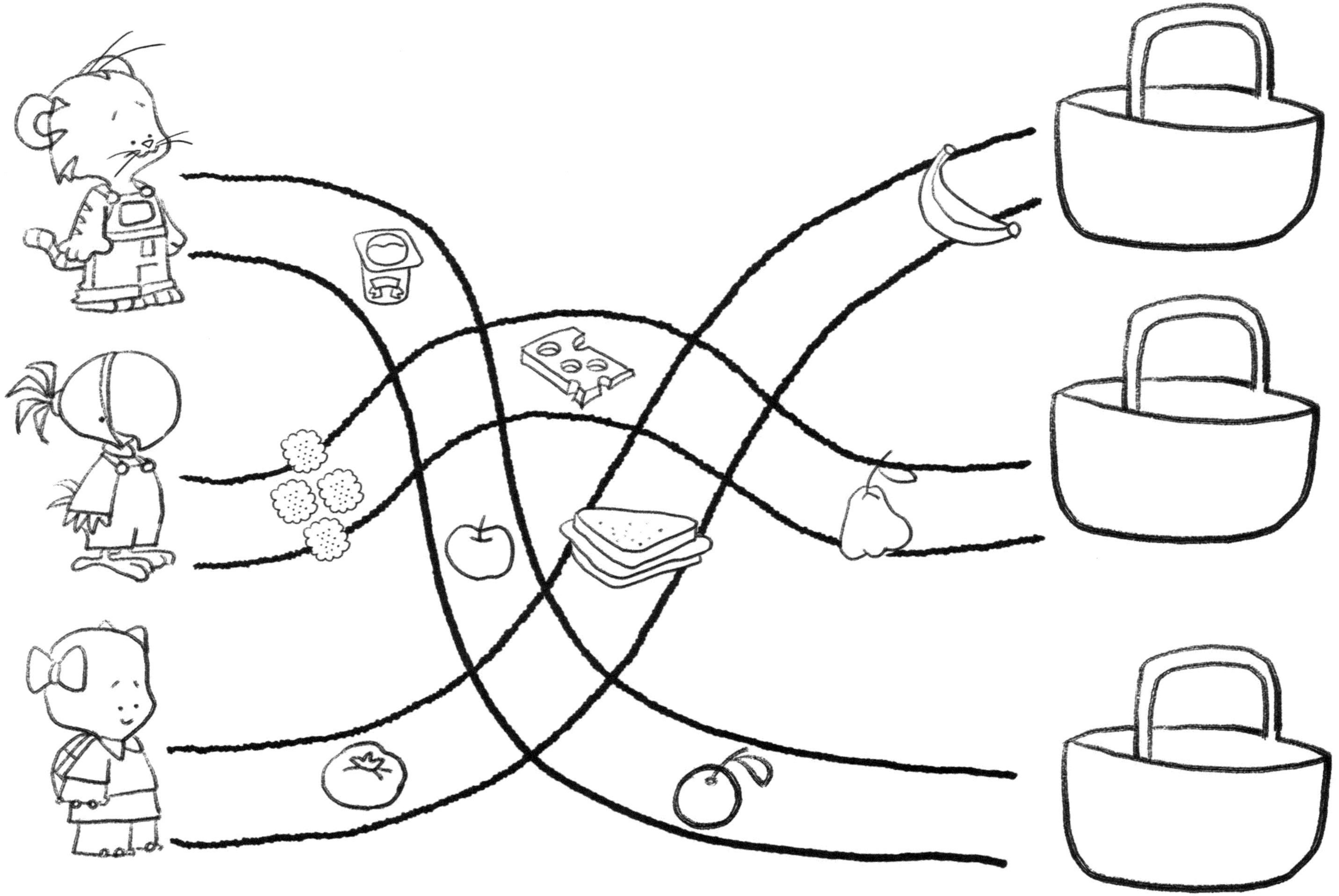

7.4

Name:

✤ Listen and trace the numbers with the correct colours. Listen and colour the spiders with the correct colours.

✤ Listen and place the stickers.

7.5

Name: _____

- Draw food from the song on the plate.
Decorate the rim of the plate by making a pattern with different stickers.

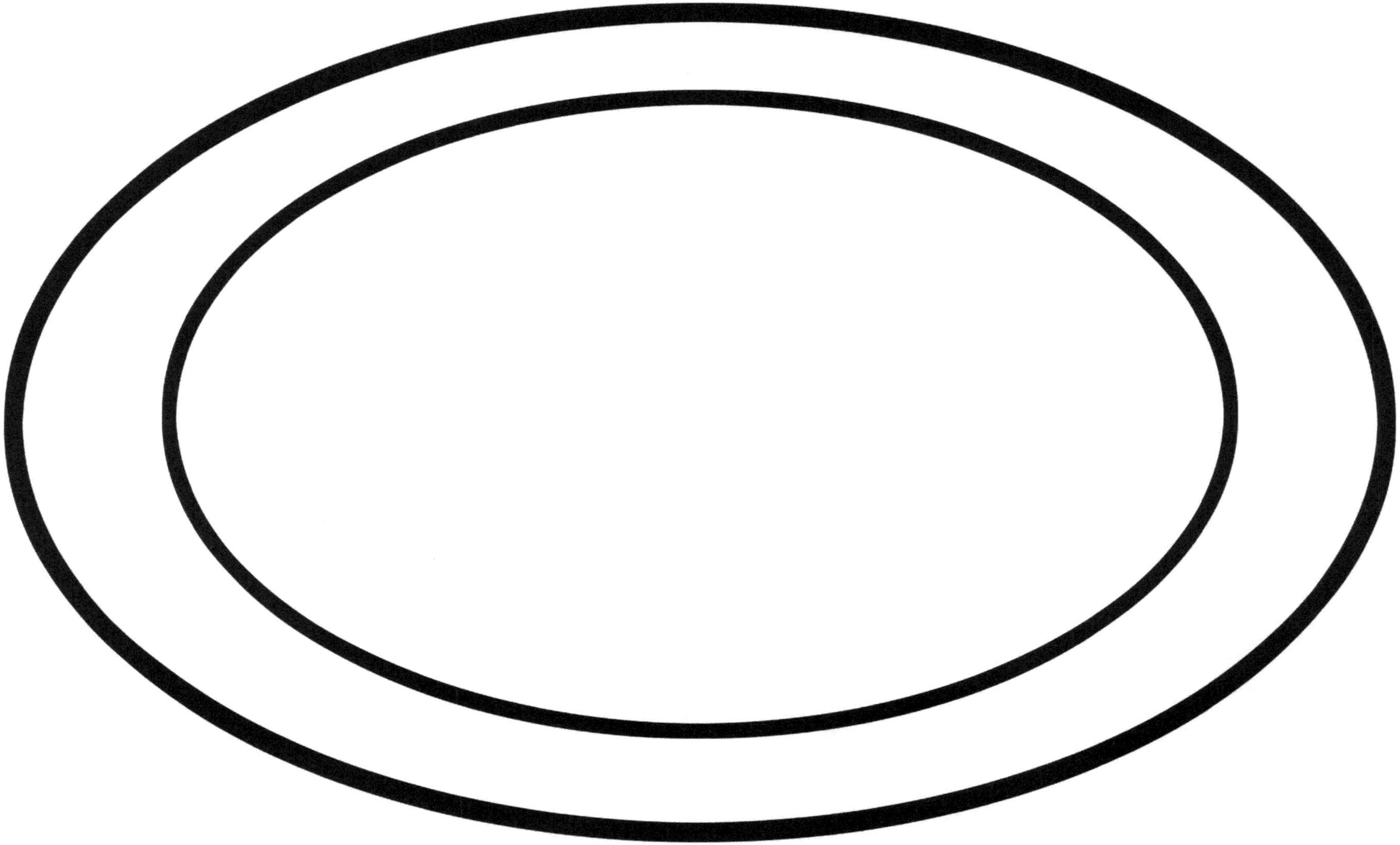

7.6

Name: _____

★ Draw smiley faces next to the healthy food and frowny faces next to the unhealthy food.

8.1

Name: _____

- Use different colours to match the animals with their shadows.

8.2

Name: ———————

★ Look at the race and write the number that corresponds to each animal.

8.3

Name: _____

● Draw a line from each animal to the place where it lives.

8.4

Name: _____

★ Listen and trace the numbers with the correct colours. Listen and colour the spiders with the correct colours.

★ Listen and place the stickers.

Name: _____

8.5

★ Draw the animals inside the old lady's tummy.

Name: _____

8.6

Draw legs on the ant, fly, spider and centipede.

9.1

Name: _____

★ Look at the patterns and draw the missing pictures.

9.2

Name: _____

★ Colour each shape on the left a different colour. Look for the shapes in the picture and then colour them using the key.

9.3

Name: _____

Draw the sun, a rainbow, the moon and some stars.

1

2

9.4

Name: _____

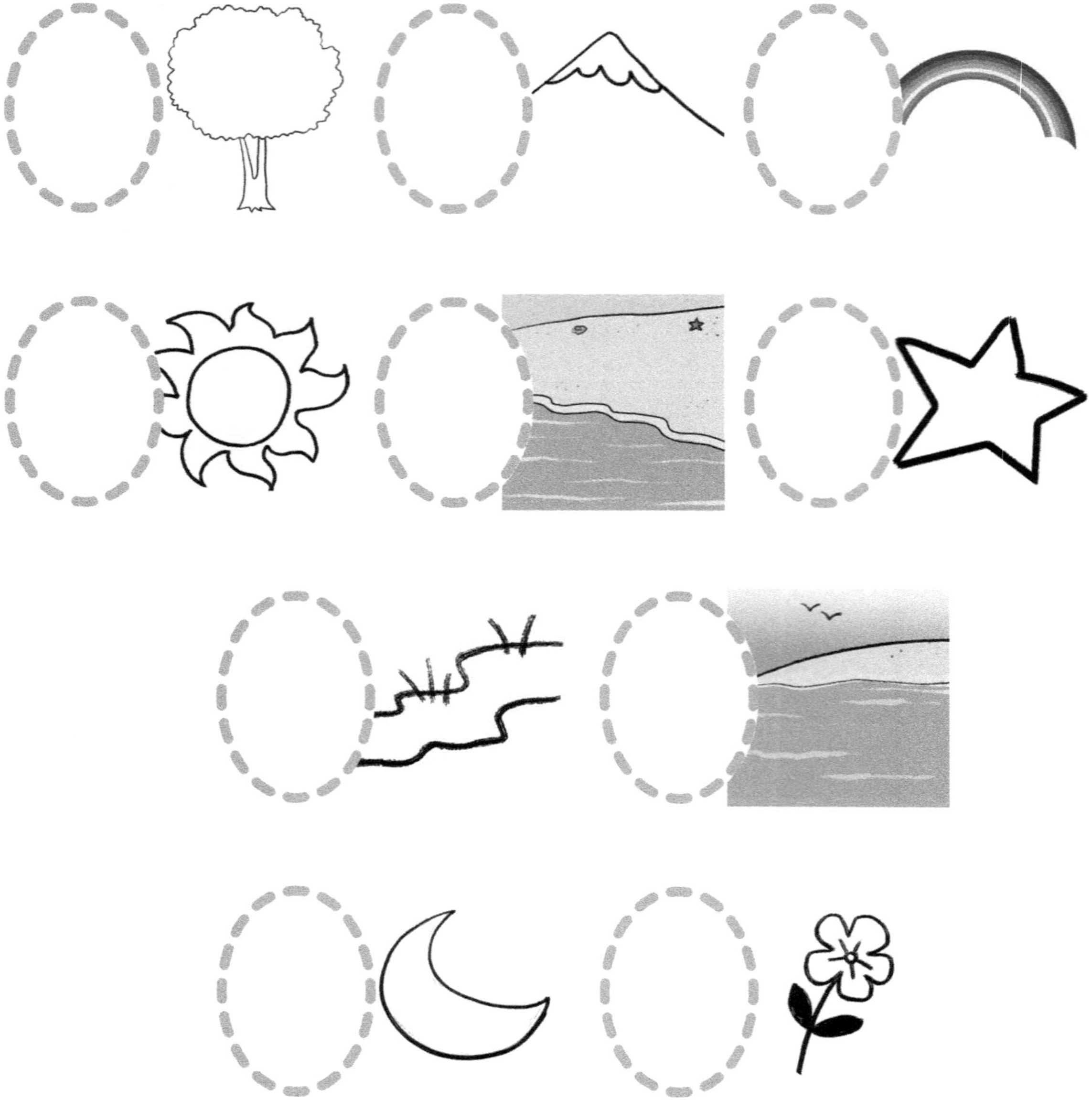

★ Listen and trace the shapes with the correct colours. Listen and draw the correct places.

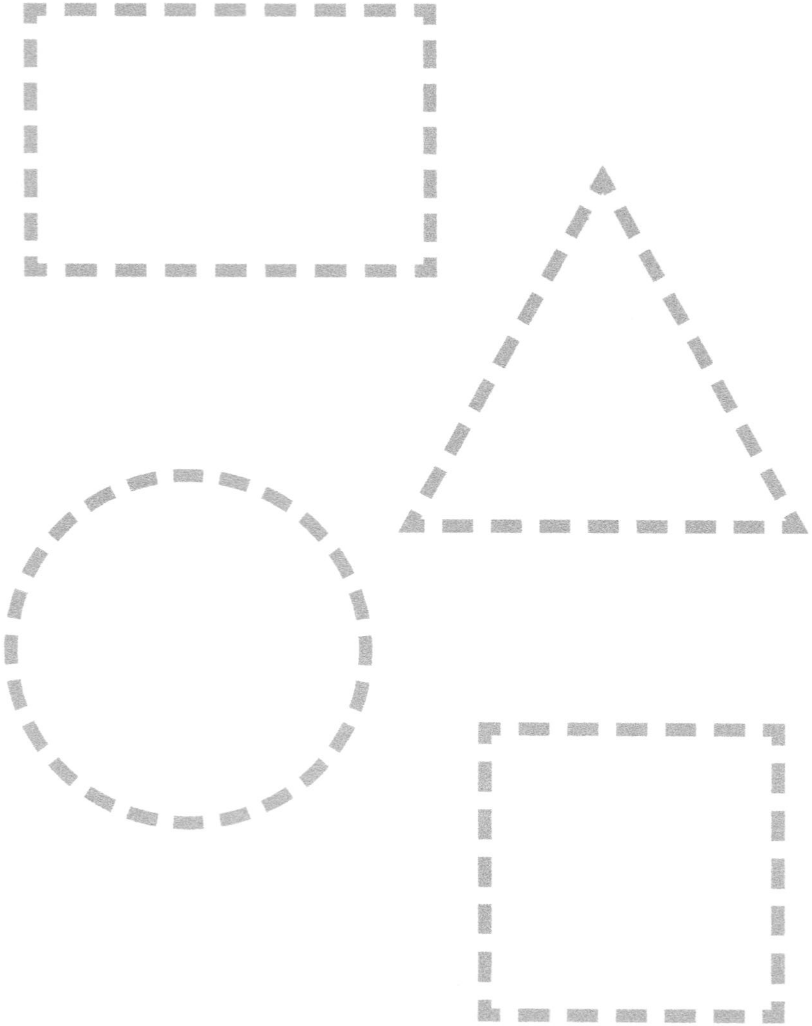

★ Listen and place the stickers.

9.5

Name: ───────────

- Colour alternate bands of the rainbow.
  Punch out the green band and glue green cellophane on the back.
  Glue crayon shavings onto the orange and purple bands.

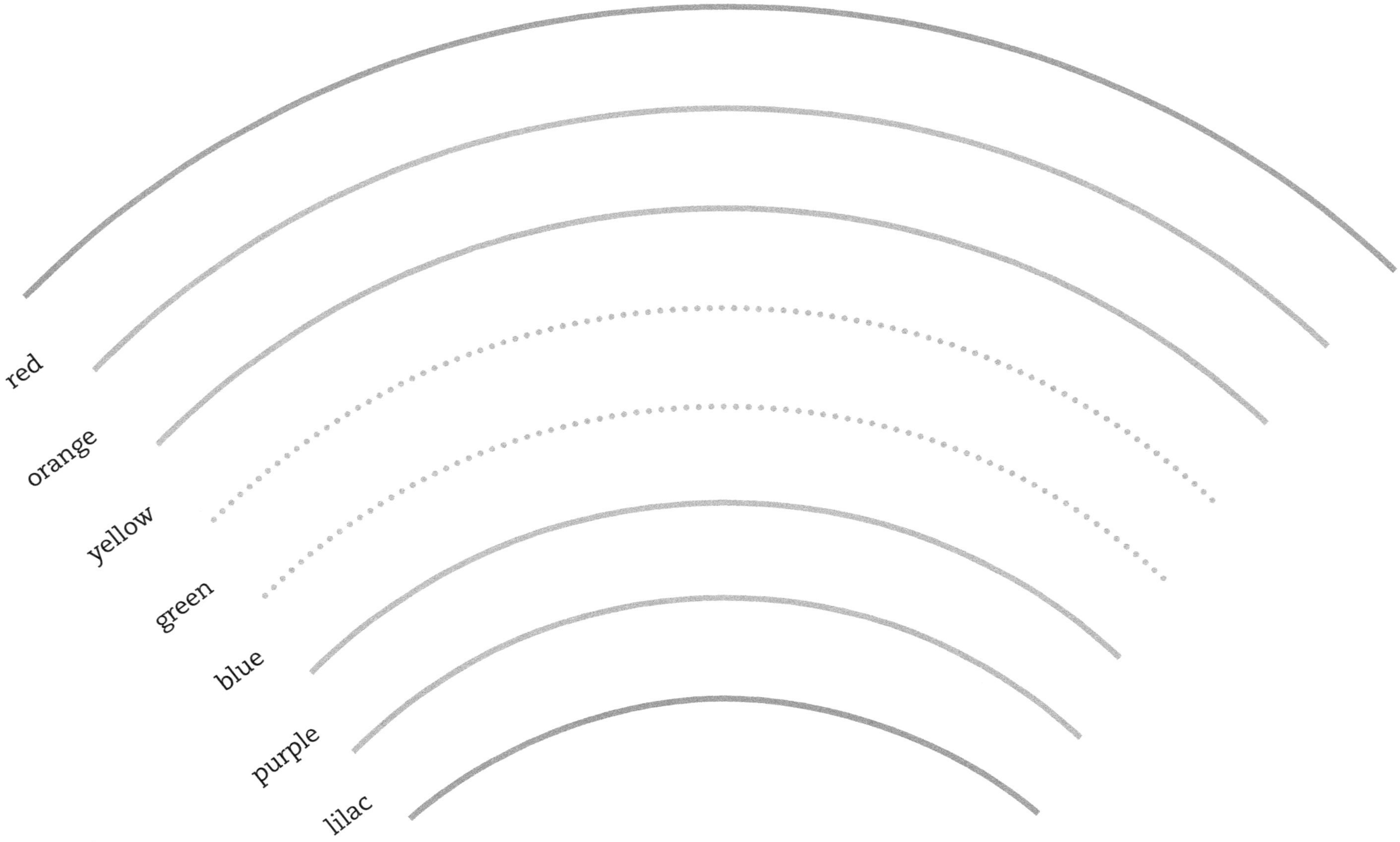

red
orange
yellow
green
blue
purple
lilac

9.6

Name: _____

★ Colour the things you see at night.

Autumn

Halloween

136

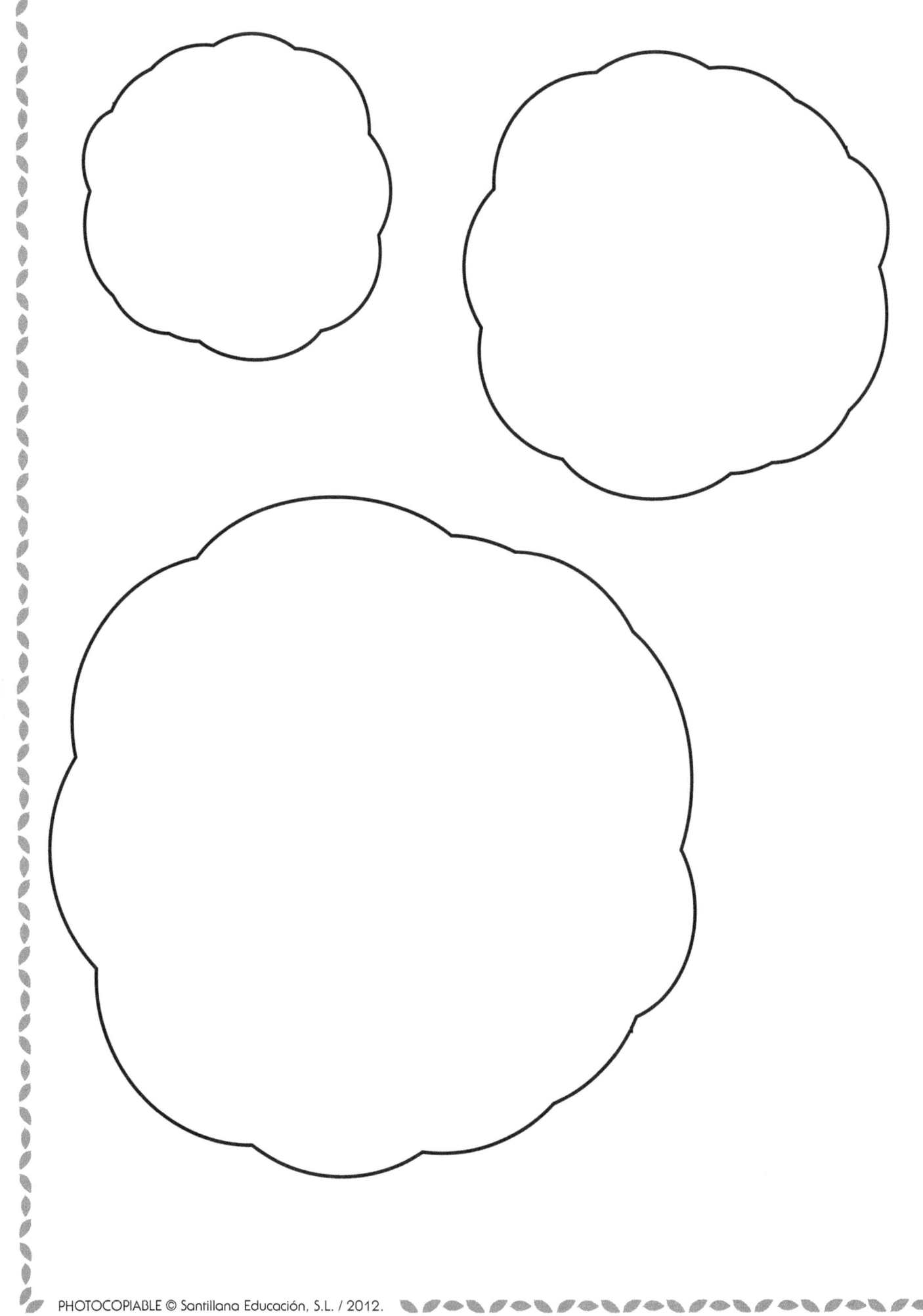

Winter

Spring

138

Easter

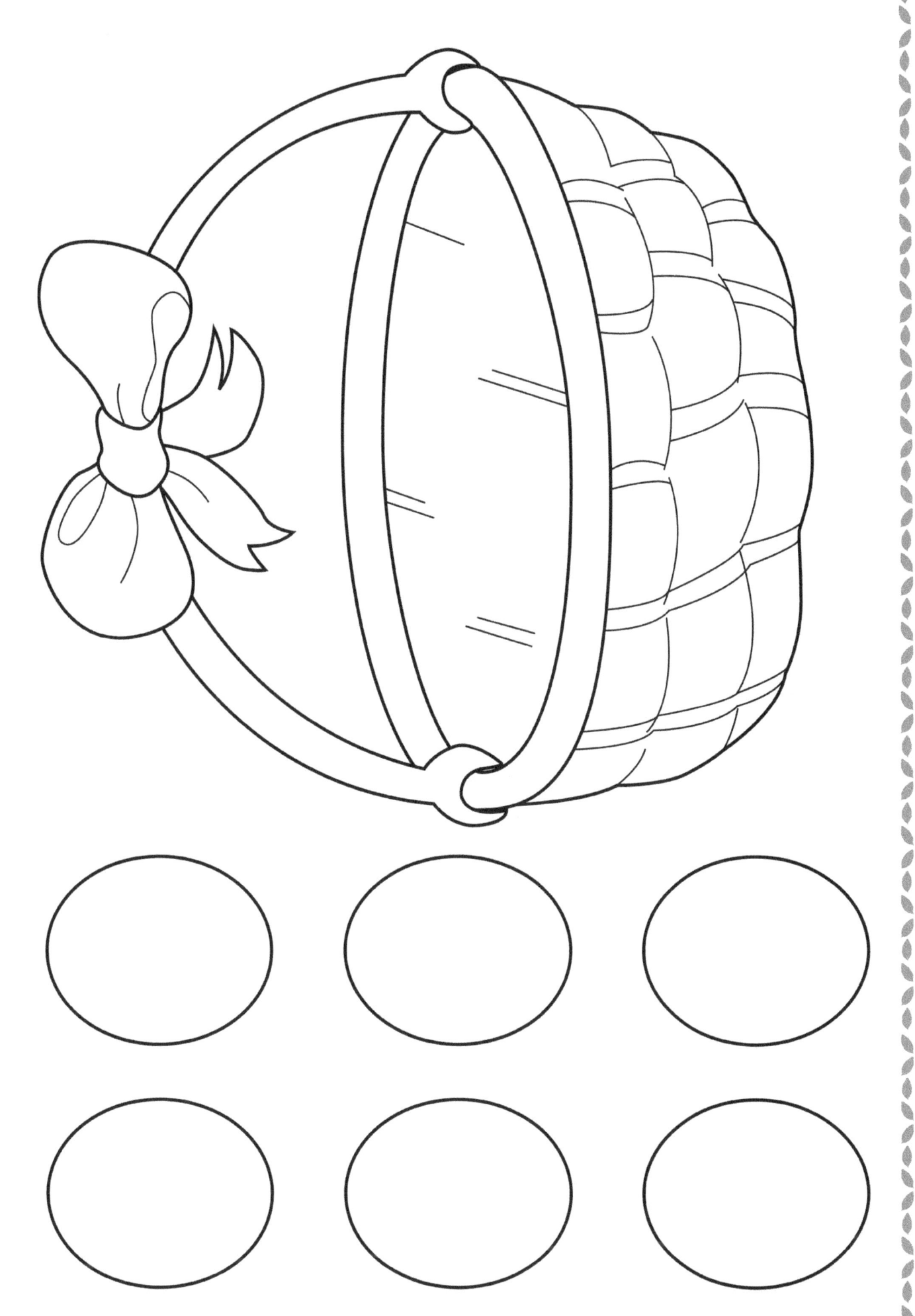

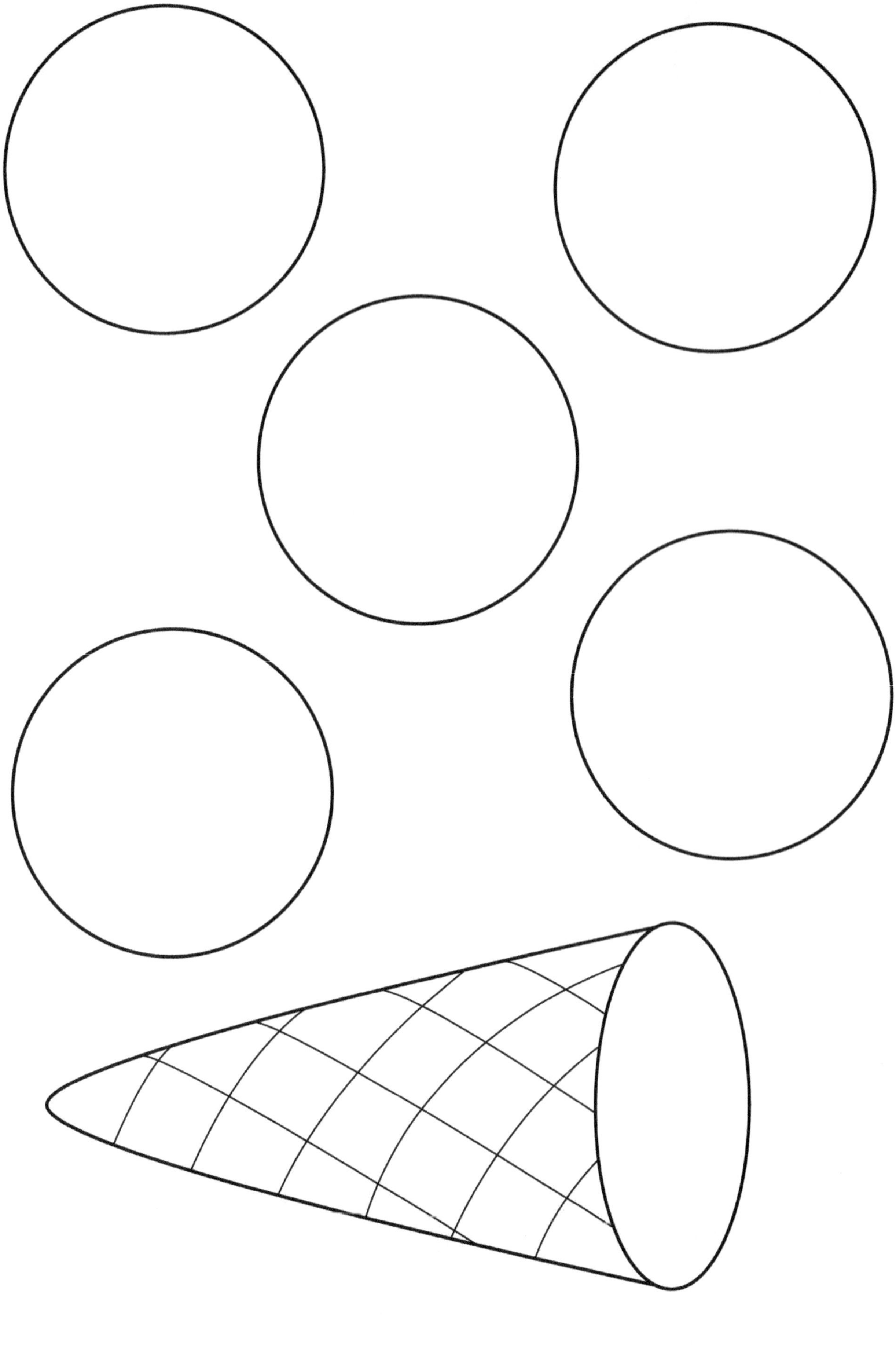

Summer

140

Big Jungle Fun 3

Well done!

Name: _____

Signed: _____

Information for parents Unit 1

❋ Unit 1

In this first unit we will be introducing your child to their English course, **Big Jungle Fun 3** and to the characters: Tommy the tiger, Tina the tortoise, Polly the parrot and the two fairies Twig and Petal.

These course characters will help to teach your child new vocabulary and concepts through songs, stories, games and fun activities which will make learning much more meaningful, entertaining and exciting.

In this unit your child will learn about the classroom, as well as reviewing the colours red, blue, yellow and green, the concepts circle and square and the numbers one to three.
The story of the unit is called: *Tina's chair*.
The authentic song is: *Tommy Thumb*.

❋ How to help your child

It is very important to have a positive attitude towards school and to show a lot of interest in what your child is learning. Your child will want to share their experiences with you. Ask them to tell you all about Tommy, Tina and Polly. Ask them how to say a word in English so that they can show you something that they have learnt in English class. It is better to point to an object and ask how to say it, rather than saying a word in their mother tongue and asking them to translate it into English.

As part of the student's material, your child has a multi-ROM with some songs and traditional stories from the course to enjoy at home. You can play the songs regularly, whilst your child is eating, in the bath or playing. This will help them to learn the songs and consequently absorb the language and use it in a natural and fun way.

Show an interest in the pop-outs and the worksheets that your child brings home or ask them to tell you what they have done or name any words they know.

Authentic song:
Tommy Thumb

Tommy Thumb, Tommy Thumb,
Where are you?

Here I am, here I am, how are you?

Peter Pointer, Peter Pointer,
Where are you?

Here I am, here I am, how are you?

Middle Man, Middle Man,
Where are you?

Here I am, here I am, how are you?

Ruby Ring, Ruby Ring,
Where are you?

Here I am, here I am, how are you?

Baby Small, Baby Small,
Where are you?

Here I am, here I am, how are you?

Fingers all, fingers all,
Where are you?

Here we are, here we are,
How are you?

Vocabulary

picture	blue
table	green
chair	one
pencil	two
rubber	three
paper	square
crayon	circle
book	school
teacher	classroom
floor	playground
yellow	writing
red	reading

For more ideas visit our website: www.richmondelt.com

Information for parents Unit 2

Unit 2

Tommy, Tina and Polly continue to help your child in their learning process, helping to make the experience enjoyable and entertaining.

In this unit your child will learn about the family, furniture and house chores, as well as reviewing more colours, the concepts circle, square and triangle and the numbers one to five.

The story of the unit is called: *Petal's family*. The authentic song is: *Five little ducks*.

How to help your child

Your child will now be more familiar with the routine of the English class and will have acquired some vocabulary and concepts. Prompt your child to say anything they can in English and to tell you about their lessons.

As part of the student's material, your child has a multi-ROM with some songs and traditional stories from the course to enjoy at home. You can play the songs regularly, whilst your child is eating, in the bath or playing. This will help them to learn the songs and consequently absorb the language and use it in a natural and fun way.

Show an interest in the pop-outs and the worksheets that your child brings home or ask them to tell you what they have done or name any words they know.

Authentic song:
Five little ducks

Five little ducks went out one day.
Over the hill and far away.
Mummy duck said, quack, quack!
But only four little ducks came back.

Four little ducks went out one day.
Over the hill and far away.
Mummy duck said, quack, quack!
But only three little ducks came back.

Three little ducks went out one day.
Over the hill and far away.
Mummy duck said, quack, quack!
But only two little ducks came back.

Two little ducks went out one day.
Over the hill and far away.
Mummy duck said, quack, quack!
But only one little duck came back.

One little duck went out one day.
Over the hill and far away.
Mummy duck said quack, quack!
But no little ducks came back.

Mummy duck went out one day.
Over the hill and far away.
Mummy duck said quack, quack!
And five little ducks came back.

Vocabulary

sofa	black
bed	white
bath	brown
brother	four
sister	five
grandad	triangle
mummy	feeding the cat
daddy	making the bed
baby	laying the table
granny	walking the dog
	watering the plants

For more ideas visit our website: www.richmondelt.com

Information for parents Unit 3

❋ Unit 3

In this unit your child will learn about the body and Christmas. They will also review the previously learnt colours, the concepts of *big* and *little*, and the numbers one to five.

The story of the unit is called: *The snowman*. The authentic song is: *The little bells of Christmas*.

❋ How to help your child

Ask your child to sing some of the songs they have heard in class. Songs are a very valuable learning tool as your child will be learning new vocabulary and concepts in a creative and enjoyable way.

As part of the student's material, your child has a multi-ROM with some songs and traditional stories from the course to enjoy at home. You can play the songs regularly, whilst your child is eating, in the bath or playing. This will help them to learn the songs and consequently absorb the language and use it in a natural and fun way.

Show an interest in the pop-outs and the worksheets that your child brings home or ask them to tell you what they have done or name any words they know.

Authentic song:
The little bells of Christmas

The little bells of Christmas
Say dong, dong, dong, dong-dong!
The little bells of Christmas
Say dong, dong, dong!
The little drums of Christmas
Say boom, boom, boom, boom-boom!
The little drums of Christmas
Say boom, boom, boom!
The triangles of Christmas
Say ting, ting, ting, ting-ting!
The triangles of Christmas
Say ting, ting, ting!
The tambourines of Christmas
Say brrring, brrring, brrring, brrring-brrring!
The tambourines of Christmas
Say brrring, brrring, brrring!

Vocabulary

hair	orange
hands	long
feet	short
nose	big
mouth	little
arm	Christmas card
leg	cracker
head	paper hat
eyes	turkey
ears	Christmas pudding

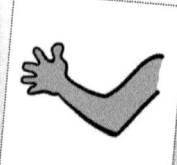

For more ideas visit our website: www.richmondelt.com

Information for parents Unit 4

Unit 4

In this unit your child will learn about toys and different forms of exercise. They will review colours, the numbers one to six and they will be introduced to the rectangle.

The story of the unit is called: *What a mess!* The authentic song is: *One finger, one thumb.*

How to help your child

Ask your child to count to six in English to help them practise what they are learning in the classes. Put out a few objects and ask your child to count them in English; also ask them what colour those objects are, as well as whether they are a circle, a square, a rectangle or a triangle.

As part of the student's material, your child has a multi-ROM with some songs and traditional stories from the course to enjoy at home. You can play the songs regularly, whilst your child is eating, in the bath or playing. This will help them to learn the songs and consequently absorb the language and use it in a natural and fun way.

Show an interest in the pop-outs and the worksheets that your child brings home or ask them to tell you what they have done or name any words they know.

Authentic song:
One finger one thumb keep moving

One finger, one thumb,
Keep moving.
One finger, one thumb,
Keep moving.
We'll all be merry and bright.
One finger, one thumb, one arm,
Keep moving.
One finger, one thumb, one arm,
Keep moving.
We'll all be merry and bright.
One finger, one thumb, one arm,
One leg, keep moving.
One finger, one thumb, one arm,
One leg, keep moving.
We'll all be merry and bright.
One finger, one thumb, one arm,
One leg, one nod of the head, keep moving.
One finger, one thumb, one arm,
One leg, one nod of the head, keep moving.
We'll all be merry and bright.

Vocabulary

robot	pink
game	purple
scooter	six
slide	rectangle
swing	climbing
bike	skipping (with a rope)
ball	playing football
dolly	cycling
teddy	swimming
monster	

For more ideas visit our website: www.richmondelt.com

Information for parents Unit 5

✤ Unit 5

In this unit your child will be learning about clothes and what they are made of. They are also going to be introduced to the prepositions *on*, *under* and the number seven.

The story of the unit is called: *I'm Tommy's parrot!*
The authentic song is: *She'll be coming round the mountain*

✤ How to help your child

Your child now knows several items of clothing in English as well as the names of some materials; ask them to tell you what they are wearing and what material they are made of. Remember to let your child express themselves in English using the language they have learnt, as they may not know or remember certain words.

As part of the student's material, your child has a multi-ROM with some songs and traditional stories from the course to enjoy at home. You can play the songs regularly, whilst your child is eating, in the bath or playing. This will help them to learn the songs and consequently absorb the language and use it in a natural and fun way.

Show an interest in the pop-outs and the worksheets that your child brings home or ask them to tell you what they have done or name any words they know.

Authentic song:
She'll be coming round the mountain

She'll be coming round the mountain when she comes.
She'll be coming round the mountain when she comes.
She'll be coming round the mountain, coming round the mountain,
Coming round the mountain when she comes.

Singing I, I yippie, yippie I,
Singing I, I yippie, yippie I,
Singing I, I yippie, I, I yippie,
I, I yippie, yippie I.

She'll be riding a white horse when she comes.
She'll be riding a white horse when she comes.
She'll be riding a white horse, riding a white horse,
Riding a white horse when she comes.

She'll be wearing pink pyjamas when she comes.
She'll be wearing pink pyjamas when she comes.
She'll be wearing pink pyjamas, wearing pink pyjamas,
Wearing pink pyjamas when she comes.

Vocabulary

socks	hat
shoes	scarf
jumper	gloves
trousers	seven
T-shirt	on
dress	under
jacket	wool
boots	cotton
pyjamas	leather

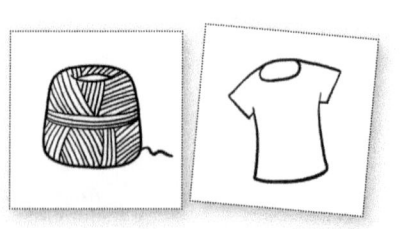

For more ideas visit our website: www.richmondelt.com

Information for parents Unit 6

Unit 6

In this unit your child will learn about places in the town and what happens after you post a letter. They will also be introduced to the concepts of *loud* and *quiet* and the number eight.

The story of the unit is called: *Tommy is a wonderful tiger!*
The authentic song is: *The wheels on the bus.*

How to help your child

It is very important to continue the learning process at home, encouraging your child to talk about school and all that they are learning. Remember that it is always better to point to an object and ask how to say it, rather than saying a word in their mother tongue and asking them to translate it into English.

As part of the student's material, your child has a multi-ROM with some songs and traditional stories from the course to enjoy at home. You can play the songs regularly, whilst your child is eating, in the bath or playing. This will help them to learn the songs and consequently absorb the language and use it in a natural and fun way.

Show an interest in the pop-outs and the worksheets that your child brings home or ask them to tell you what they have done or name any words they know.

Authentic song:
The wheels on the bus

The wheels on the bus go round and round,
Round and round,
Round and round.
The wheels on the bus go round and round,
All day long.

The wipers on the bus go swish, swish, swish...

The bell on the bus goes ring, ring, ring...

The horn on the bus goes toot, toot, toot...

Then at night the bus goes to sleep,
Goes to sleep, goes to sleep.
Then at night the bus goes to sleep,
All night long.

Vocabulary

hospital	plane
school	loud
shop	quiet
police officer	eight
fire fighter	letter box
doctor	letter
car	post man
bus	post office
train	post box

For more ideas visit our website: www.richmondelt.com

Information for parents Unit 7

❋ Unit 7

In this unit your child will learn about food and healthy eating. They will be introduced to the number nine and the prepositions *in* and *next to*. They will also review the ten colours learnt so far and the numbers one to eight.

The story of the unit is called: *Wash your hands, please.*
The authentic song is: *Today is Monday.*

❋ How to help your child

Name a type of food and ask your child whether it is good for you or not. You can also ask them about what food they like or don't like, always encouraging them to say things in English. Ask them if they can remember the story and what they should do before they eat anything.

As part of the student's material, your child has a multi-ROM with some songs and traditional stories from the course to enjoy at home. You can play the songs regularly, whilst your child is eating, in the bath or playing. This will help them to learn the songs and consequently absorb the language and use it in a natural and fun way.

Show an interest in the pop-outs and the worksheets that your child brings home or ask them to tell you what they have done or name any words they know.

Authentic song:
Today is Monday

It's dinner time!

Today is Monday.
Monday green beans.
All you hungry children,
Come and eat it up!

Today is Tuesday.
Tuesday spaghetti.
Monday green beans.
All you hungry children,
Come and eat it up!

Today is Wednesday.
Wednesday soup.
Tuesday spaghetti.
Monday green beans.
All you hungry children,
Come and eat it up!

Today is Thursday.
Thursday fish.
Wednesday soup.
Tuesday spaghetti.
Monday green beans.
All you hungry children,
Come and eat it up!

Today is Friday.
Friday pizza.
Thursday fish.
Wednesday soup.
Tuesday spaghetti.
Monday green beans.
All you hungry children,
Come and eat it up!

Today is Saturday.
Saturday chicken.
Friday pizza.
Thursday fish.
Wednesday soup.
Tuesday spaghetti.
Monday green beans.
All you hungry children,
Come and eat it up!

Today is Sunday.
Sunday ice cream.
Saturday chicken.
Friday pizza.
Thursday fish.
Wednesday soup.
Tuesday spaghetti.
Monday green beans.
All you hungry children,
Come and eat it up!

Vocabulary

cheese
ham
tomato
pizza
biscuit
sandwich
yoghurt
apple
banana

pear
buns
sweets
crisps
nuts
fruit
in
next to
nine

For more ideas visit our website: www.richmondelt.com

Information for parents Unit 8

Unit 8

In this unit your child will learn about wild and farm animals, and they will be introduced to the number ten as well as the prepositions *in front of* and *behind*. They will review the vocabulary for animals, colours, prepositions and numbers one to nine.

The story of the unit is called: *I'm sad! I'm grumpy! I'm sleepy!*
The authentic song is: *There was an old lady who swallowed a fly.*

How to help your child

Your child has now covered numbers one to ten. Use every opportunity to ask them to count objects around them, as well as to tell you what colour objects are. Remember to point at things rather than just naming objects.

As part of the student's material, your child has a multi-ROM with some songs and traditional stories from the course to enjoy at home. You can play the songs regularly, whilst your child is eating, in the bath or playing. This will help them to learn the songs and consequently absorb the language and use it in a natural and fun way.

Show an interest in the pop-outs and the worksheets that your child brings home or ask them to tell you what they have done or name any words they know.

Authentic song:

There was an old lady who swallowed a fly

There was an old lady who swallowed a fly.
I don't know why she swallowed a fly, oh why, oh why?

There was an old lady who swallowed a spider.
It wiggled and wiggled and tickled inside her.
She swallowed the spider to catch the fly.
I don't know why she swallowed a fly, oh why, oh why?

There was an old lady who swallowed a bird.
She swallowed the bird to catch the spider,
That wiggled and wiggled and tickled inside her.
She swallowed the spider to catch the fly.
I don't know why she swallowed a fly,
Oh why, oh why?

There was an old lady who swallowed a cat.
She swallowed the cat to catch the bird.
She swallowed the bird to catch the spider,
That wiggled and wiggled and tickled inside her.
She swallowed the spider to catch the fly.
I don't know why she swallowed a fly,
Oh why, oh why?

There was an old lady who swallowed a dog.
She swallowed the dog to catch the cat.
She swallowed the cat to catch the bird.
She swallowed the bird to catch the spider,
That wiggled and wiggled and tickled inside her.
She swallowed the spider to catch the fly.
I don't know why she swallowed a fly,
Oh why, oh why?

Atchooooooooo...!
Out came the dog, the cat, the bird, the spider and the fly...
Goodbye. Goodbye fly.

Vocabulary

lion	chicken
bear	butterfly
monkey	fly
cat	spider
fish	ladybird
dog	bee
cow	in front of
pig	behind
sheep	ten

For more ideas visit our website: www.richmondelt.com

Information for parents Unit 9

❊ Unit 9

In this unit your child will learn about the natural world and the differences between night and day. They are going to review numbers, colours, shapes and prepositions.

The story of the unit is called: *Magic sky*. The authentic song is: *I can sing a rainbow*.

❊ How to help your child

This is the last unit and the summer holidays are approaching, your child is going to spend a long time away from their English teacher. If possible, maintain as much contact as possible with the language through songs, TV, stories and so on. Always encourage your child to enjoy learning and not make it a chore; use their natural enthusiasm for the world around them as a tool for practising their vocabulary and knowledge.

As part of the student's material, your child has a multi-ROM with some songs and traditional stories from the course to enjoy at home. You can play the songs regularly, whilst your child is eating, in the bath or playing. This will help them to learn the songs and consequently absorb the language and use it in a natural and fun way.

Show an interest in the pop-outs and the worksheets that your child brings home or ask them to tell you what they have done or name any words they know.

Authentic song: I can sing a rainbow

Red and orange and yellow and green,
Violet and purple and blue.
I can sing a rainbow,
Sing a rainbow,
Sing a rainbow too.

Look with your eyes,
Listen with your ears,
And sing everything you see.
I can sing a rainbow,
Sing a rainbow,
Sing along with me.

Red and orange and yellow and green,
Violet and purple and blue,
I can sing a rainbow,
Sing a rainbow,
Sing a rainbow too!

Vocabulary

rainbow	tree
star	sun
moon	day
mountain	night
sea	firework
beach	bat
river	owl
flower	

For more ideas visit our website: www.richmondelt.com

Big Jungle Fun 3   Evaluation Term 1

Name: _____

Class: _____ Date: _____

Teacher: _____

English

- [ ] Shows an interest in learning.
- [ ] Understands and follows instructions in English.
- [ ] Understands and responds in a non-verbal manner.
- [ ] Understands and responds in a verbal manner.
- [ ] Takes part in activities.
- [ ] Understands important words.
- [ ] Can say some words in English.
- [ ] Enjoys songs and chants.
- [ ] Joins in with songs and chants.
- [ ] Enjoys stories.
- [ ] Listens carefully to stories.
- [ ] Joins in with important phrases from the story.
- [ ] Joins in with reenactments of the story.

Concepts

- [ ] Understands the difference between big and small.
- [ ] Recognises and can name the colours yellow and red in English.

General

- [ ] Pays attention in class.
- [ ] Respects the classroom rules.
- [ ] Can identify the characters from the course.
- [ ] Completes work with care.
- [ ] Completes work independently.
- [ ] Likes to play games.
- [ ] Cooperates with others.
- [ ] Tries hard.

Comments: _____
_____
_____
_____

| A | always | NA | nearly always | S | sometimes | NY | not yet |

Big Jungle Fun 3   Evaluation Term 2

Name: _____

Class: _____   Date: _____

Teacher: _____

English

- [ ] Shows an interest in learning English.
- [ ] Understands and follows instructions in English.
- [ ] Understands and responds in a non-verbal manner.
- [ ] Understands and responds in a verbal manner.
- [ ] Takes part in activities.
- [ ] Understands important words.
- [ ] Can say some words in English.
- [ ] Can say some phrases in English.
- [ ] Enjoys the songs and chants.
- [ ] Joins in with songs and chants.
- [ ] Enjoys stories.
- [ ] Listens carefully to stories.
- [ ] Joins in with the important phrases from the story.
- [ ] Joins in with reenactments of the story.

Concepts

- [ ] Can say the numbers one and two in English.
- [ ] Can count up to two objects.
- [ ] Recognises the numbers one and two.
- [ ] Can write the numbers one and two.
- [ ] Understands the difference between big and small.
- [ ] Recognises and can name a geometric shape: the circle.
- [ ] Recognises and can name the colours yellow, red and blue in English.

General

- [ ] Pays attention in class.
- [ ] Respects the classroom rules.
- [ ] Can identify the characters from the course.
- [ ] Completes work with care.
- [ ] Completes work independently.
- [ ] Likes playing games.
- [ ] Cooperates with others.
- [ ] Tries hard.

Comments: _____
_____
_____
_____

| A | always | NA | nearly always | S | sometimes | NY | not yet |

Big Jungle Fun 3   Evaluation Term 3

Name: _____

Class: _____ Date: _____

Teacher: _____

English

- [ ] Shows an interest in learning English
- [ ] Understands and follows instructions in English.
- [ ] Understands and responds in a non-verbal manner.
- [ ] Understands and responds in a verbal manner.
- [ ] Participates in activities.
- [ ] Understands important words.
- [ ] Can say many words in English.
- [ ] Can say some phrases in English.
- [ ] Enjoys songs and chants.
- [ ] Joins in with songs and chants.
- [ ] Enjoys stories.
- [ ] Listens carefully to stories.
- [ ] Understands the stories.
- [ ] Joins in with the important phrases in the story.
- [ ] Joins in with the reenactments of the story.

Concepts

- [ ] Can say the numbers up to 3 in English.
- [ ] Can count up to 3 objects.
- [ ] Recognises the numbers 1 – 3.
- [ ] Can write the numbers 1 – 3.
- [ ] Understands the difference between big and small.
- [ ] Recognises and can name a geometric shape, the circle.
- [ ] Recognises and can name the colours yellow, red, blue and green in English.

General

- [ ] Pays attention in class.
- [ ] Respects the classroom rules.
- [ ] Completes work with care.
- [ ] Completes work independently.
- [ ] Likes playing games.
- [ ] Cooperates with others.
- [ ] Tries hard.

Comments: _____

| A | always | NA | nearly always | S | sometimes | NY | not yet |

Big Jungle Fun 3

Term 1

Name:

Term 2

Big Jungle Fun 3

Name: _____

Big Jungle Fun 3

Term 3

Name:

Big Jungle Fun 3

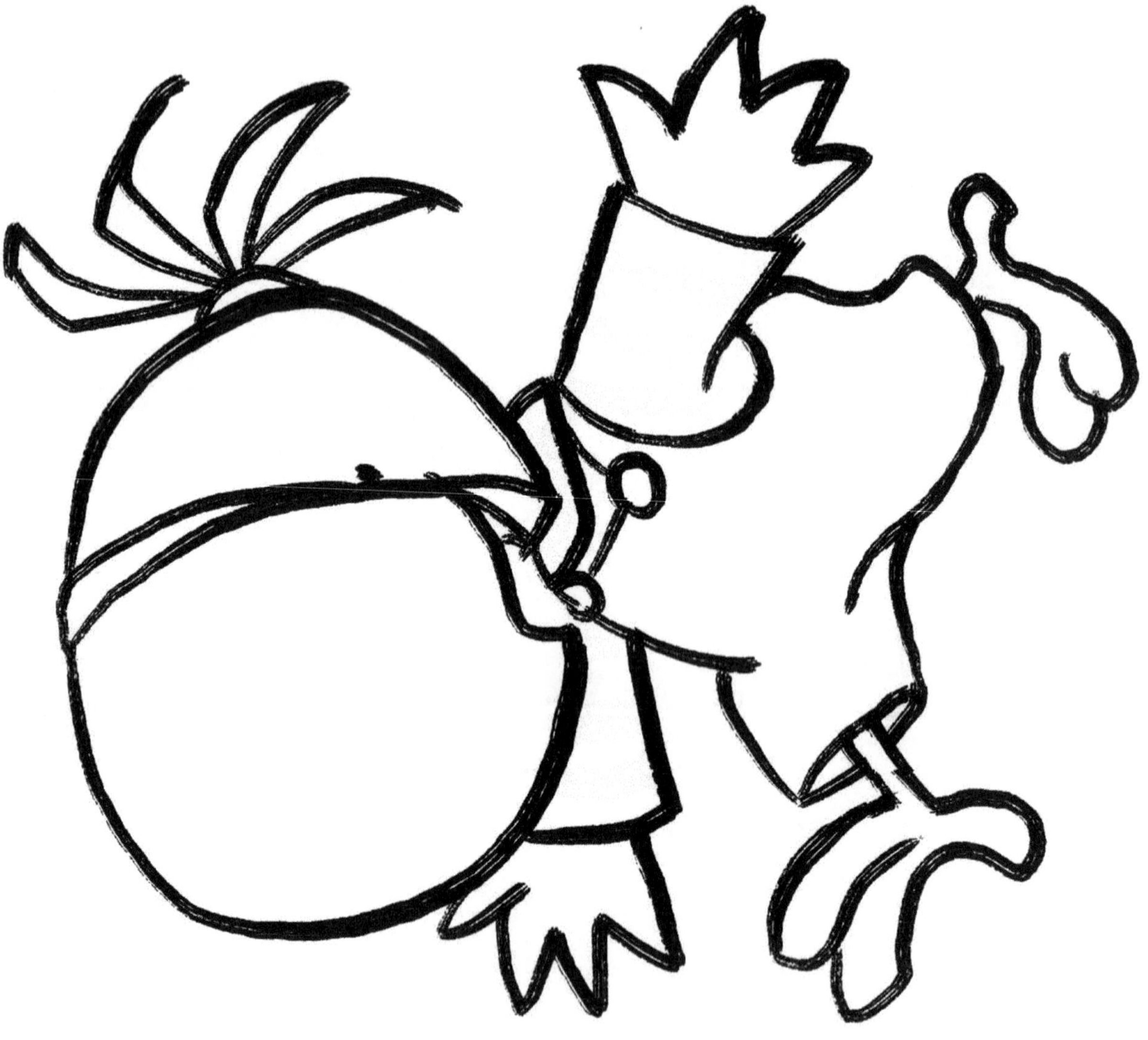

Big Jungle Fun 3

Notes